GLOW PUCKS

AND 10-CENT

BEER

Beer Night (AP Photo/Cleveland Press, Paul Tepley)

GLOW PUCKS AND 10-CENT BEER

The 101 Worst Ideas in Sports History

GREG WYSHYNSKI

TAYLOR TRADE PUBLISHING
Lanham • New York • Boulder • Toronto • Oxford

Published by Taylor Trade Publishing
An imprint of The Rowman & Littlefield Publishing Group, Inc.
4501 Forbes Boulevard, Suite 200, Lanham, Maryland 20706

Distributed by NATIONAL BOOK NETWORK

Library of Congress Cataloging-in-Publication Data

Wyshynski, Greg, 1977–
   Glow pucks and 10-cent beer : the 101 worst ideas in sports history /
   Greg Wyshynski.— 1st Taylor trade publishing ed.
        p. cm.
     ISBN 1-58979-308-0 (pbk. : alk. paper)
     ISBN 978-1-58979-308-8
     1. Sports. I. Title.
   GV583.W97 2006
   796.09—dc22   2005025904

♾™ The paper used in this publication meets the minimum requirements of American National Standard for Information Sciences—Permanence of Paper for Printed Library Materials, ANSI/NISO Z39.48-1992.

Manufactured in the United States of America.

Taking dinosaurs off this island is the worst idea
in the long, sad history of bad ideas.

—DR. IAN MALCOLM,
The Lost World: Jurassic Park

CONTENTS

CONTENTS

CONTENTS

CONTENTS

CONTENTS

ACKNOWLEDGMENTS

SPECIAL THANKS to Sarah Greenblatt, Mary Kimm, Jimmy Patterson, Ken Moore, Dulcie Wilcox, Laura Wyshynski, and Andrew Stanger for their assistance, both professionally and personally.

This book is dedicated to Bob and Pat Wyshynski—who not only made me but made me a sports fan.

INTRODUCTION

LIKE MANY children of suburbia, I grew up playing the Atari 2600, marveled by computer graphics that today aren't as sophisticated as the digital readout on most microwave ovens. In 1982, Atari was set to take over the home video-game world with *E.T., the Extra-Terrestrial*, a cartridge based on the box-office smash directed by Steven Spielberg. Gamers all over America were getting the shakes in anticipation of what was assumed to be the best-selling title in the history of the industry.

Then it finally came out. And it sucked. Really hard.

I remember playing the game, teary eyes fixated at the debacle on my television, jaw slacked to the ground in ghastly astonishment. *They made E.T. green! Why does every screen look the same? It doesn't even follow the plot of the movie!*

Atari sold so few of its *E.T.* games that it ended up burying millions of them in a desert in New Mexico. The company lost $100 million on the title and $536 million overall in 1983.

How the hell could this happen? How could such a sure thing go wrong? Later in life, I found out that the game designers only had 40 days to create *E.T.* because Atari's ownership promised Spielberg that the game would come out before Christmas. That left the designers precious little time for such frills as—oh, I don't know—making the game playable without making the players feel the desire to gouge their own eyes out with an ice-cream scoop.

That's the practical answer. But the *E.T.* game was guilty of so much more, such as taking the fan base for granted, being a victim of its own hype, and, most important, defying the basic tenet of its medium—providing entertainment. For the same reasons, sports have yielded their own titanic blunders and miscalculations over the years. The title of this book should really be *The 101 Worst Ideas, Notions, Inventions, Conceptions, Trends, Decisions, and Traditions in Sports History.* But then there wouldn't have been any room on the cover for my gigantic Ukrainian last name.

In researching this book, I noticed some commonalities between the subjects. Greed and avarice motivated many of these blunders, from overexpansion and overexposure to pay-per-view sports to the 1994 baseball strike. Some decisions sought to simplify rules that ended up becoming even more chaotic, which is why instant replay causes so many migraines and why a Caribbean soccer tournament's points system forced two teams to score on their own nets (and defend their opponents' own goals) to qualify for the championship finals. Some innovations were a direct insult to the essence and culture of the sports in which they were introduced—from the logic-defying tradition of the coin toss to the overtime shootout, which manages to undermine an entire game's worth of team play.

Mostly, the chapters in this book tell stories of unchecked narcissism and egomania: Donald Trump's sacrificing the USFL to secure an NFL expansion team; celebrities' attempting to "cross over" into other mediums, for example, nonsingers taking on the national anthem or models/actresses posing as sideline "reporters"; major league teams' attempting to juice their attendance through irresponsible promotions such as 10-Cent Beer Night and Disco Demolition Night, both of which ended with fan riots.

INTRODUCTION

The entries are categorized by sport and subject. The top 25 worst ideas in sports history are presented in list form at the end of the book. They are ranked according to how egregious, embarrassing, and damaging they were to the parties involved; how idiotic the factors were behind the failures; and, above all else, whether they were a direct insult to the basic institutions of the sports they influenced.

Ideally, this list will make you laugh, think, laugh again, ponder what these people were thinking, perhaps chuckle, contemplate our place in God's plan, belly-laugh, and then make you buy about a dozen more copies to give to friends, use as coasters, what have you. Thank you for reading.

ADVENTURES IN EGOMANIA

PART 1

Hulk Hogan, Thespian

Like Brando . . . Only with 24-Inch Pythons

WHEN TERRY BOLLEA, aka Hulk Hogan, made his feature-film debut in *Rocky III*, it was all well and good. He played a wrestler called "Thunderlips," a character whose name might have been better suited for Sylvester Stallone's first film, the 1970 porno *The Party at Kitty and Stud's*. (Guess which character Sly played . . .)

Thunderlips participates in a hybrid boxing/wrestling match with the Italian Stallion to open *Rocky III*. The joke was, of course, that Hogan was playing a thinly veiled version of his World Wrestling Federation persona. Moviegoers enjoyed the scene, assuming that the Hulkster had gotten the acting thing out of his system and would return to body-slamming the Iron Sheik at basketball arenas around the country. Little did they know that this would mark the beginning of an appalling film career that would span well into the next decade.

No Holds Barred (1989) was Hogan's first starring vehicle. Coproduced by WWF owner Vince McMahon, it offered the Hulkster a chance to show his range as an actor. For example, instead of playing a professional wrestler named "Hulk Hogan," he plays one named "Rip Thomas." Eat your heart out, Meryl Streep!

After that movie flopped, Hogan returned in 1991's *Suburban Commando*, in which he portrayed a muscle-bound alien who crash-lands on Earth and joins a family headed by dad Christopher Lloyd and mom Shelley Duvall. Two hours of their wedding night would have made for a more interesting movie.

Mr. Nanny (1993) finds Hogan playing a washed-up wrestler (another stretch) put in charge of protecting a pair of children from kidnappers. For a kids' movie, it is rather barbarous: the *Home Alone*–style comedy is only slightly less violent than Hulk's bloody Wrestlemania 2 steel-cage match with King Kong Bundy.

Hogan's action/adventure television show *Thunder in Paradise* (costarring Chris Lemmon, after his father, Jack, presumably passed on the project) came and went. That set the stage for Hulk's *Citizen Kane* of awful movies: *Santa with Muscles* (1996). In what is considered one of the worst films ever made, Hogan plays a curmudgeonly health-food guru who gets knocked unconscious while wearing a Santa suit (don't ask). He wakes up believing he's jolly ole St. Nick and saves an orphanage from real estate developer Ed Begley Jr., who wants the priceless crystals that are buried underneath the building (I beg of you, don't ask).

This film—nay, the entire Hulkster canon—reaffirms once and for all that, as an actor, Hulk Hogan was one hell of a professional wrestler.

Manute Bol, Hockey God
Like a Really, Really Tall Version of Alexandre Daigle

STANDING SEVEN-FEET, seven-inches tall and weighing about as much as one of Dennis Rodman's feathered boas, Manute Bol went from a native of Sudan to a record-setting NBA veteran of 11 seasons. He set the mark for blocked shots by a rookie, with 397 in 1984, and had over 2,000 in his career. Bol also holds the record for having the three-point shot that most resembled projectile vomit.

After his playing days were over, he gave up big-and-tall clothing endorsements and potential costarring roles in Billy Crystal movies to return to the Sudan, where a civil war was raging. Bol spent millions of dollars supporting the opposition movement against the Islamic government. After the Sudanese government promised to sign several peace treaties in the mid-1990s, Bol agreed to take a job with the ruling body. Unfortunately, he discovered that the job was his only if he renounced Christianity and converted to Islam. He refused and was subsequently forbidden from leaving the country. He and his family eventually bribed their way to Egypt and then returned to the United States in 2002.

Bol made it his mission to use whatever celebrity he had in the States to raise funds for his organization, the Ring True Foundation, which supported young boys who lost their parents in the Sudanese war. His first opportunity came on the FOX network's *Celebrity Boxing* special, which featured Z-level stars pummeling each other. Bol won by decision over former Chicago Bear William "Refrigerator" Perry and donated the purse to the Sudanese refugees.

At least Bol threw a few punches as a boxer. For his next fund-raising stunt, the big guy gained even more publicity for his cause but ended up embarrassing a minor league team and its fans by never actually performing as an athlete.

The Central Hockey League's Indianapolis Ice—known for in-rink sumo matches and pink jerseys for Valentine's Day—signed Bol to a contract and announced that he would appear against the Amarillo Gorillas on November 16, 2002. The team found a uniform for his lanky frame and had men's 16.5-sized skates shipped in. The game would mark the first time in which Bol wielded a stick that didn't have a lion impaled at the end of it. (To be sure, Bol did kill a lion with a spear at 15 years old, something that his agent actually used in contract negotiations.)

But Manute never exactly hit the ice for the Ice; rather, he sat on the bench until his chronic rheumatoid arthritis flared up and his feet swelled in the skates. At that time, he took them off and walked to the locker room in bright white socks via a black mat laid on the ice. By the end of the first period, he was out of uniform and signing autographs in the arena. Bol's tenure with the team ended after the game.

A season-high crowd of 5,859 came to Conseco Fieldhouse for the bait and switch, which added to Bol's charitable coffer. One year later, Bol came back to Indiana for another fund-raising event, this time suiting up as a jockey at Hoosier Park racetrack. He never actually got on a horse.

Jeff Gordon Hosts
Saturday Night Live
NASCAR Star Leaves Millions Begging
for Sinead O'Connor's Return

SPORTS ARE an important part of *Saturday Night Live* history . . . although not as important as unfunny reoccurring characters that eventually spin off into financially disastrous feature films.

Fran Tarkenton, Bill Russell, and O. J. Simpson hosted in the late-night comedy show's early years. Joe Montana told America he was going "upstairs to masturbate" in a memorable sketch from 1987. Wayne Gretzky spoofed Elvis Presley movies in the 1989 opus *Waikiki Hockey*. Michael Jordan portrayed the first black Harlem Globetrotter, "Sweet River" Baines, in a 1991 sketch.

Athletes could be counted on to play against type and provide self-deprecating laughs. Even Yankees owner George Steinbrenner caused chuckles in Studio 8-H when, as the manager of a grocery store, he simply saw no benefit in firing employees.

On January 11, 2003, NASCAR champion Jeff Gordon joined the pantheon of athletes turned *SNL* hosts. He should have stayed in the pit. The monologue was promising, as the writers wisely chose not to put laughs in the walking lug nut's hands; they allowed cast members Rachel Dratch and Chris Parnell to spoof NASCAR fans—and the host—from the audience. Then Gordon was forced into action, playing a zookeeper in his first sketch—which stunk like the bottom of a monkey's cage. Jeff may have noticed how painfully tedious the sketch was had he taken his eyes off the cue cards. Next, our racing hero played a jet pilot talking to students on Career Day. Goose's corpse from *Top Gun* would have been more animated. You knew that the *SNL* writers had no clue what to do with a talentless host when they cast him as a waiter and as the sympathetic husband that gets one or two laughless lines.

Was Gordon the worst host in *SNL* history? Yeah, probably. But he did have his defenders, such as a message-board poster named "Lynn from San Diego" on AmericanRaceFan.com: "I give him an 'A' for clearly looking relaxed and enjoying himself. Not many professional acotrs *[sic]* pull off the level of cool that he portrayed."

Rafael Palmeiro for Viagra
Baseball All-Star Pulls a Boner

ANSWER: Pizza and beer. Aerosmith and Run DMC. Male sexual potency drugs and sports fans.

QUESTION: Uh, what are matches made in heaven, Alex?

VIAGRA WAS the first erectile-dysfunction product to explode into sports advertising. After Bob Dole became the American face of male sexual impotence (no wonder he lost to Bill Clinton), NHL Hall of Famer Guy LaFleur played the same role in Canada. In 2001, Viagra extended a sponsorship to NASCAR's Mark Martin and his No. 6 car, forever taking away "It's because Jeff Gordon won the pole" as a bedroom excuse for Southern gentlemen. Interest in Viagra really swelled once its maker began pumping advertising into MLB broadcasts and when one of the game's biggest stars was thrust into an ad campaign.

By 2002, Texas Rangers first baseman Rafael Palmeiro had 447 home runs and 1,470 RBIs; in other words, he was the last guy who you figured had trouble scoring. Yet Viagra thought that the 37-year-old was perfect to push those little blue pills. (Then again, everything is bigger in Texas, right?)

The slugger wasn't shy about being the athletic face for erectile dysfunction. "I guarantee you, everybody in this clubhouse has tried it," Palmeiro told *Tribune News Service*, "and most are asking me for it."

Makes you wonder how many athletic supporters they went through in the Rangers' locker room that season.

No word if Palmeiro's will be the first plaque in Cooperstown that can double as a coat rack . . . that is, if he ever gets to Cooperstown. In August 2005, Palmeiro went from being the poster boy for erectile dysfunction to the public face of baseball's steroid scandal. Turns out, Raffy needed a little help with his other bat, too.

Will voters still elect the Viagra spokesman to the Hall of Fame? It's a hard decision, but I assume that they'll be up for the task.

Deion Sanders Releases *Prime Time*

Finally, a Reason to Hammer a Railroad Spike into Your Ear

I N THE 1990s, the line between musicians and athletes got as blurred as David Wells's vision after 30 beers. Garth Brooks wanted to be an outfielder for the San Diego Padres. Rapper Master P pursued a minor-league basketball career. Meanwhile, Shaquille O'Neal cut enough rap albums to issue a "best of" in 1996; former NBA player Wayman Tisdale released four blues/jazz albums; even boxer Oscar de la Hoya and soccer player Alexi Lalas dropped records by the end of the decade.

But the *Abbey Road* of horrific athlete-turned-musician albums came from multisport star "Neon" Deion "Prime Time" Sanders. His 1994 album, the cleverly titled *Prime Time*, was a combination of rap and R&B, all of it in the key of tone-deaf.

The most popular track from the CD was Sanders's autobiographical lament "Must Be the Money," in which we learn how difficult life can be for a multimillionaire who won both a World Series and a Super Bowl. It is my intention to share some of Mr. Sanders's prose with you, keeping in mind his delivery often slurred his lyrics to the point where it sounded like he was singing through a burlap gag.

"Must Be the Money" begins with what can only be described as "porno guitar." We're in a good groove for about half a second before our crooner chimes in with this insightful lyric (again, I will do my best to get this down word for word):

Well all-rye . . . yeh-ya.

We have now arrived at the first stanza, which is a spoken-word essay about Deion's early days as a professional football player:

You know, ever since I turned pro in 1989 / When I signed on the dotted line / It was strange / Cause things changed / For the better / And for the worse / So I called my muh-ma / And she said, "Bay-bee."

At this point, I'm sure we're all thinking she said, "Make a crappy rap album, son." But, thanks to a gaggle of generic female backup singers, we discover what she actually told him:

Muss be da money / (Deion: "Yeah, yeah, yeah, yeah") / Muss be da mon-aye / (Deion: "Iss got to be, because I got people wanna be my friend") / Muss be da money / (Deion: "People I never knew. People I never even thought about asso-she-ating with") / Muss be da mon-aye / (Deion: "I don't know what it is. Talk to me. Check it ow.")

And with that, we're into the "singing" portion of the song. Deion actually sounded a lot like R. Kelly . . . if R. Kelly had all of his teeth and his tongue removed and was administered a powerful horse tranquilizer. I will do my best to transcribe what this marble-mouth sang:

Down and relax / With gators on my feet / I get some pretzels every day of the week / (Deion's background-singing doppelganger: "In my hair") / My hair is dark / My fingernails too / Six packs are down'in and I don't know what to do / Muss be da mone.

"Da mone?" Vic Damone? Ah, who knows . . .

Are those really the lyrics? Of course not. But I never sent in those five Ovaltine labels to get the "Prime Time Decoder Ring" in the mail.

We get through two more "Muss be da money" choruses, in which Deion boosts about the cars and the planes and the women he rides (although not at the same time). Later, we learn how Prime Time hits Da Club:

Flashin' lights / On the dance flow / The DJ says my name as I make my intro / (Dopple-Deion: "And you know") / The place is packed / Nowhere to find a seat / But Prime don't worry / Cause I sits in VIP / Muss be da mone / (Ladies: "Muss be da money") / I got so much jewels / (Ladies: "Muss be da mon-aye") / Twenty-six with all his dudes / (Ladies: "Muss yadda yadda") / To afford the way I live / (You know who: "You know what") / The Pepto Bismol's at my crib.

The aforementioned made me give up this futile attempt to transcribe the poetry of Deion Sanders, because his mush-mouth delivery and Seussian rhyme make it humanly impossible. Yet I stayed until the end of "Must Be the Money" and was surprised to find this positive and uplifting send-off from P. T. Sanders:

The furss thing people say is / "Prime, don't let money change ya. Don't let money change ya" / I say, "Hey—Don't let money change you" / Because personally, iss gonna change my address / My phone number / My wardrobe / Hey, my snakeskin shoes gonna change into gators / My library card gonna change into a credit card . . .

With that, the generic ladies singing backup, the porno guitar, and Prime Time himself begin to fade out after four minutes, eight seconds of auditory torture. And all we're left to ponder is: Deion Sanders actually had a library card?

STRIKEOUTS AND ERRORS

PART 2

The Legalized Spitball

"He should be in the Hall of Fame with a tube of KY Jelly attached to his plaque."

—Former MLB manager Gene Mauch, on pitcher and noted spitballer Gaylord Perry

IF YOU'RE over a century old, chances are that you're going to appear a little different from how you did when you were born. I mean, look at Cher . . .

Baseball's no exception. At one time, getting a runner out meant drilling him with the ball. Foul territory didn't exist when baseball began, which must have made being a catcher an interesting experience. And as incredible as this may sound, at one point in baseball history, African Americans weren't even allowed in the major leagues! (Don't say that you didn't learn anything new by reading this book.)

Time passes, attitudes change, and so do the rules of any organized sport. For instance, beginning in the late 19th century, baseball pitchers were allowed to basically do anything that they wished to do with the ball. Emery boards, slippery elm, tobacco juice, chewing gum, resin, talcum powder, paraffin, and good ol' fashioned saliva were used to alter the surface of the ball. The emery ball and the spitball were both incredibly effective, allowing the ball to dip and curve in a manner so unnatural that a NASA astrophysicist couldn't have predicted its flight pattern.

Like any artificial enhancement in Major League Baseball (*see* steroids, anabolic), mediocre players became all-stars thanks to the shiner, spitter, and scuffer. But critics argued that the pitchers' actions didn't just give them a competitive advantage—throwing an abraded or lathered ball also put them at greater risk of injury and endangered hitters and fielders who were unprepared for the irregular nature of the ball's course.

The emery ball was the first to go, sometime during the 1910–1920 period. In December 1919—after, shall we say, a challenging season for baseball—the National League's rules committee voted to ban the spitball, and the American League followed suit. Yet both leagues added an inexorably idiotic caveat to their rulings: the ban would be applied to *new* spitball pitchers. Hurlers that had been using the slop ball could continue to do so as long as their teams reported them as spitballers to Major League Baseball each season. American League teams could report two pitchers apiece; National League clubs had an unlimited number of spitball slots available. That's right: as long as you tell baseball that your pitcher is cheating, he can continue cheating!

The plan originally called for the total ban of spitballs by the 1921 season (ironic, when you consider that the baseballs went from spit to juice during the decade). But in 1920, the leagues decided to permit 17 "grandfathers" to continue to use the illegal pitch because their spitballing had predated the ban. So despite the fact that any pitcher who entered the league after 1920 was prohibited from throwing a spitball, the Sloppy 17 were allowed to proceed with their phlegmy artistry.

In 1934, the final legal spitball pitcher—Burleigh Grimes of the Pittsburgh Pirates—retired at the age of 41, ending the era of MLB-sanctioned cheating (that is, until baseball's drug-testing "policy" later in the century).

Randy Johnson
Nicknamed the "Big Unit"
What? . . . Was the "Split-Fingered Schvantz" Already Taken?

KNOW WHY they called Pete Rose "Charlie Hustle"? Because the man hustled. Know why they called Robert Moses Grove "Lefty"? Because he was left-handed. So why, dear Lord why, did pitching great Randy Johnson get saddled with a nickname like the "Big Unit"?

Blame former Montreal Expo Tim Raines. Randy Johnson, in an interview with the *Montreal Gazette*, said that Raines bumped into him while walking out of the batting cage, looked up, and said, "You're a big unit." Teammates repeated the nickname for the 6-feet-10 Johnson until it stuck. But what possessed a guy such as Raines, with a badass nickname like "Rock," to stick a burgeoning young star with a nearly lewd nickname like the "Big Unit" for the rest of his career? Why not something cool, like "Dr. Death" or "Stone Cold"? During Johnson's career, the left-hander could have easily been given a better nickname than the "Big Unit." For example,

THE KRUK KILLER: In the 1993 all-star game, Johnson faced Philadelphia's John Kruk. He fired the first pitch over Kruk's head, and the rotund Phillies slugger—fearing for his life—flailed at the next three pitches to meekly strike out.

THE BIRDINATOR: In a 2001 spring-training game, Johnson killed a dove that had the misfortune of flying in front of home plate as his fastball flew in.

REDNECK MCMULLET: C'mon, have you ever seen the guy?

Want further proof that this nickname is the worst in baseball history? In 2004, the New York Yankees attempted to trade with the Los Angeles Dodgers and the Arizona Diamondbacks to bring Randy Johnson to the Bronx. The initial deal fell through, so the Yankees and Diamondbacks worked out a trade on their own.

Can't you hear the sports report now? "The three-way didn't go as planned, but they still found a way to take in the Big Unit . . ."

Yikes!

Impersonating the Other Team's Manager
The "Prince of Pranks" Strikes Out

THERE WERE only three truly noteworthy things about Moe Drabowsky as a major league pitcher. The first was an 11-strikeout relief performance in Game 1 of the 1966 World Series for eventual champion Baltimore. The second was the fact that he was a native of Poland. But most important of all, Drabowsky was baseball's "Prince of Pranks," pulling practical jokes over 17 seasons with six different teams.

Indeed, Drabowsky may have been a one-man precursor to MTV's *Punk'd*. He put live goldfish in opponents' water coolers. He gave baseball commissioner Bowie Kuhn a "hotfoot," a gag in which the victim's shoe is lit on fire, usually via a matchbook stuck to the heel with chewing gum. Then there was the time that Moe tried to toss an M-80 into the teepee of Atlanta Braves mascot Chief Noc-A-Homa and, of course, the snakes that he dropped into Brooks Robinson's locker and Luis Aparicio's pants.

Every good prop comic has his weapon of choice. Gallagher wielded the watermelon-bashing Sledge-O-Matic; Moe Drabowsky had the bullpen telephone. He sometimes used it to call long-distance or to order fast food during a game. But his most notorious prank came in the 1960s, featuring the bullpen phone, an opposing pitcher, and Kansas City A's manager Alvin Dark.

With Jim Nash pitching a shutout for the home team late in the game, Drabowsky called the Kansas City bullpen from the Baltimore pen's phone. He did his best impression of Dark, asking that a relief pitcher begin to warm up. Nash soon glanced over at the pen, saw a teammate throwing during his shutout performance, and lost his cool. The Orioles finally broke through against the shaken starter and eventually won the game.

OK, so it was a great prank. But what if the reliever hurt his arm while warming up for no reason? What if that loss actually had meant the difference between making and missing the postseason? Not to mention the fact that Drabowsky's behavior did nothing to shatter certain stereotypes associated with Polish Americans . . .

Marge Schott Remains Owner of the Reds
Call It the "Pennant Racism"

*O**n occasion in this book, it becomes imperative to share an extraordinary point of view on a given theme. The only way to truly accomplish that is by appointment of a guest essayist on said topic. This is one such instance.***

Woof, woof! It's me, the ghost of Schottzie 2!

In my canine former life, I was the successor to Schottzie, the unofficial mascot of the Cincinnati Reds and furry life-mate to eccentric owner Marge Schott. After Schottzie went to the big doghouse in the sky in 1991, it was me and Marge for the next decade.

Oh, Marge. What a card! I used to love it when she would accidentally drop cigarette ashes on my back, causing several small fires to spark. "Hot dog! Getcher hot dog here!" she'd yell, using one of her several dozen copies of *Mein Kampf* to stamp out the flames.

I know, I'm just the ghost of a Saint Bernard and thus no expert, but I still can't believe that the powers-that-be in Major League Baseball let mommy own the Reds for 15 years. I guess things were OK for the first eight or so. I remember hearing how Schottzie used to run around and "make" all over the outfield turf, so things couldn't have been all that bad, right?

But the kibbles sure did hit the bits around 1992. That's when former Reds marketing director Cal Levy said in a deposition that Marge used to call former players Eric Davis and Dave Parker her "million-dollar niggers." He also testified that Marge had a Nazi swastika armband in her home; she corroborated the story. Again, I'm just a dead dog, but it'd be logical to think that baseball would figure out a way to get this chain-smoking racist Nazi sleeper agent out of its ownership ranks.

Yet baseball decided to let her keep the Reds, though in 1993 it fined her $25,000 and suspended her for one year after her "racially and ethnically offensive" comments. She was to undergo sensitivity training in that year away from the Reds.

Mommy came back in 1994 to take over the Reds again. In May, she showed the world that her time away from baseball had made her incredibly open-minded. Instead of just going after blacks, now she was attacking gays, too. She told the *Cincinnati Enquirer* that she didn't want her players wearing earrings "because only fruits wear earrings."

In 1996, Mommy made a few more mistakes. And unlike mine, you couldn't clean them up by laying an old newspaper on top of them.

Umpire John McSherry died on the field during the first inning of the Reds' home opener that year. The game was postponed, but Mommy disagreed with the decision. "I feel cheated. This isn't supposed to happen to us, not in Cincinnati," she said, prompting many to wonder if she actually was on a first-name basis with the grim reaper. She sent flowers to apologize for her comments, but according to the *Dayton Daily News*, they had been regifted from a television station's flowers to the team.

Later in 1996, she repeated comments that she had made earlier in the decade about some German guy named Adolf: "Everybody knows he was good at the beginning but he just went too far," she told ESPN. Oops. That was bad. Even worse, she had taken her notorious cost cutting (Marge used to recycle office supplies) to new heights—she dumped the out-of-town scoreboard at Riverfront Stadium to save $350 a month.

The baseball people had heard and seen enough. They took away day-to-day operation of the Reds from her for two years beginning in 1996. By 1999, she sold her controlling interest in the Reds for $67 million.

Mommy died in March 2004 at the age of 75. That's only 10.7 in dog years . . .

Umpires' Ever-Changing Strike Zone

Killing the Ump Would Only Make Him Stronger

I SOMETIMES imagine what touring the Museum of Modern Art would be like if accompanied by a Major League Baseball umpire.

We'd be standing in front of Georges-Pierre Seurat's 1886 oil painting *Evening, Honfleur.* I would join a crowd of onlookers in marveling at Seurat's ability to liken the breakwater with the cloud formations in order to symbolize the transient relationship between humanity and nature. Then my umpire friend would anticipate a break in the conversation and exclaim that it was, without a doubt, the greatest ice sculpture of William Howard Taft that he had ever seen.

My point is that umpires have the innate ability to view something completely different from what everyone else sees—from the players in the batter's box, on the pitching mound, in the infield and the outfield to the fans in the lower level, the mezzanine, the upper deck, even including that guy who's always ready outside the stadium with a shopping cart full of toasted pretzels.

This isn't due to some optical deficiency—as much as we fans would like to believe it, I don't think that professional sports leagues are in the practice of hiring blind men to officiate their games . . . Americans with Disabilities Act be damned. Umpires just survey life a little differently than you or I do.

How else can you explain Eric Gregg's strike zone in Game 5 of the 1997 National League Championship Series, which was wider than his eyes at a 24-hour all-you-can-eat hamburger buffet? The rules are pretty clear about pitches needing to actually *cross* the plate to be counted as strikes; the final pitch from Florida's Livan Hernandez to Fred McGriff appeared to be closer to the left-field foul pole than to the Atlanta Braves slugger.

The major league strike zone has been officially defined only 13 times since 1876. The general rule has always been, as MLB claimed in 1969, that "the strike zone is the space over home plate which is between the batter's armpits and the top of his knees when he assumes his natural stance." Pretty straightforward, right? Well, in 1988 baseball confused the matter by ruling that the "upper limit" of the strike zone is "a horizontal line at the midpoint between the top of the shoulders and the top of the uniform pants." Now, instead of just worrying about taking a foul ball in the twig and berries, umpires had to break out a protractor just to figure out what constitutes a strike. The zone was altered again eight years later, when the "lower limit" was moved to the bottom of the knees.

Major League Baseball's rule tweaks helped foster the inconsistency that ran rampant during the 1990s, when pitchers felt squeezed by the strike zone and batting statistics reached record levels. But it still doesn't change the fact that the strike zone is baseball's answer to Anna Nicole Smith: average one day, enormous the next. That's the umpires' fault.

What's the solution? Baseball nearly found one with the computerized QuesTec system, which rated umpires' ability to manage the league-mandated strike zone. But the technology was as imperfect as the human beings operating it, and umpires varied their strike zones from the QuesTec parks to the parks that didn't have the technology. Still, the computerized rating system was a good first step toward sucking the subjectivity out of major league umps.

Replacing Gum with a $264K Jersey

After Bust, Baseball Card Makers Go Bonkers

THE FIRST thing that you always hear from a baseball-card collector is some sob story about how he ripped up a 1951 Willie Mays rookie card in the spokes of his Schwinn or how his mother trashed his cache of cards while he was attending community college.

Psychologists call this "suppression." These whimsical tales are defense mechanisms for the colossal desolation that is the collector's life, in light of the fact that he—or, hail Freud, his mother—treated millions of dollars in sports memorabilia as most people treat a soiled tissue.

Of course, no one knew how much those packs of chalky gum with cards inside were going to be worth some day. There were no price guides, card shows, or late-night pitchmen on the Home Shopping Network shrieking about how this Pedro Martinez card is better than your Pedro Martinez card because it's "a Grade 10, near mint-to-mint, factory-sealed limited edition investment!"

There has always been this winking acceptance of gimmickry between baseball-card makers and consumers. We've always known that we get 10 Howie

Koplitz cards before we get 1 Mickey Mantle. We're pretty sure that the Billy Ripken error card from 1989 (when he had "f—k face" written on the bottom of his bat) and that 2003 Brandon Puffer/Jung Bong card from Topps were—ahem—simple editorial oversights. And we understand that packs cost $9 a pop because of the high-gloss technology being utilized. (OK, so we aren't exactly sold on that last one.)

When it became apparent that fans would put up with a little snake oil, the card companies just couldn't help themselves. Soon, we didn't simply have one factory set of cards annually from each manufacturer; we had about seven, with names such as "Fleer Authentix" and "Topps Chrome Baseball Series One." When companies ran out of computer-generated graphics and bloated design, they started putting out "retro" sets that looked just like the cards your mother threw away, only this time you were paying out the ass for them.

In the 1990s, when the poststrike baseball memorabilia industry crashed, the card companies just went insane. They started putting shards of game-used bats into cards. They started stitching game-worn uniforms, gloves, and balls into cards. Some fans ate this up, feeling a personal connection with their favorite ballplayers by owning a few millimeters of material. It's the same vinculum that I feel when I go to the stadium and take a deep breath, knowing that somewhere mixed in with the oxygen and pollen might just be a few of Mike Piazza's snot molecules.

All of this game-worn gimmickry was well and good until October 2003, when cardmaker Donruss announced that it was slicing up an authentic Babe Ruth 1925 New York Yankees jersey for insertion into 2,100 packs of cards over the next three years. It had purchased the jersey at an auction for $264,210 the previous summer. Cries of "desecration" came from purists who were outraged that one of only three known Ruthian pinstriped jerseys was getting reduced to one-inch squares for a publicity stunt. Hall of Fame catcher Gary Carter, invited to shill by Donruss at its press conference, said, "It would be different if this were the only Ruth jersey in existence, but it's not."

In a related story, the Louvre denied that there were plans in place to chop up the Mona Lisa into spitball-sized pieces and to hand them out to the first 3,000 visitors this year.

Letting Batters Call Their Own Pitches
AKA Really, Really, Really Shrinking the Strike Zone

REMEMBER playing kickball in gym class? There were only three constants from playground to playground:

1. The red rubber ball would either be too inflated or filled with just enough air to keep it from looking like a shriveled cherry.
2. Two best friends would declare themselves a "package deal" when teams were being chosen to ensure they would not compete as rivals. It seemed pretty peculiar at the time, until Paul Kariya and Teemu Selanne pulled the same trick in the NHL's 2003 off-season.
3. Absolutely, positively, *no spinners!*

Spinners were those balls that could not be kicked with any power or purpose of direction. The pitcher would palm the ball, spin his wrist, and apply a tight rotation as he rolled it. Any player brave enough to battle a spinner would boot either a harmless pop-up or, more likely, a weak grounder for an out. The beauty of kickball was that a player at the plate had complete control over what pitches were headed his or her way. Don't like the look of a ball? Call it a "do-over," pick it up, toss it back. Upon spying a spinner rolling toward home, a kicker could simply snatch it off the ground and return it to the pitcher, declaring, "Hey, dude, whadideye tell you: *No spinners!*"

Typically, a pitcher would oblige, his semilegal strategy to dominate the game thwarted. But sometimes the spinning wouldn't stop. I've seen shrewd players pick up seven consecutive balls in a single "at foot."

Incredibly, baseball used to look a whole lot like kickball in the 1870s. *Beadle's Dime Baseball Player*, a rules handbook published in 1876, describes a Major League Baseball regulation that allowed batters to call for one of three pitches of their liking: high (waist to shoulders), low (one foot off the ground to the waist), or "fair ball" (between one foot off the ground and the shoulders). The batter would tell the umpire, who would then tell the pitcher where to throw the pitch; after the request was made, it could not be altered.

Since the breaking ball wasn't in common use yet, hitters were basically allowed to ask for a fastball high or low. The practice was commonplace until 1886, when a joint rules committee between the rival National League and the American Association of Base Ball Clubs agreed to eliminate the option for batters to call for the location of their pitches.

Bill James, one of baseball's greatest historians, has a positive take on the ancient rule: "In some respects [it is] like a football team calling for a run or a pass," he writes in *Historical Baseball Abstract* (2001), "but in another sense [it] can be seen as a reflection of one of baseball's unique features: It is the only sport in which the team that has the ball is on defense."

The White Shorts
Veeck Dresses Chicago in Bermuda

IN THE MID-1970s, the Chicago White Sox had an identity crisis. Bud Selig nearly purchased them and shipped the team to Milwaukee but opted to relocate the one-season-and-done Seattle Pilots instead. The financially troubled team was then in talks to head west, replacing the Pilots in the Queen City. Chicago didn't want to go without its Sox, so city leaders turned to former owner Bill Veeck and helped him buy the team.

In 1976, Veeck put his eccentric stamp on the ballclub with uniforms that could be called "unique" . . . if "unique" actually meant "hideous." The Sox traded in their pinstripes for white nylon pullover jerseys with a large V-neck collar. The lettering of "Chicago" on the front looked straight out of 1890, which would have been retro chic had it not been for the fact that the jersey itself looked straight off the bargain rack in a Sears men's sleepwear department. You know your team's a fashion disaster when they look more at home on a tobacco card next to Honus Wagner than on broadcast television.

"Now that was a bad uniform," Rickey Henderson once told *Sports Illustrated*. "I wouldn't play in that uniform." (This coming from a guy who played for both the couture-challenged Oakland A's and San Diego Padres. . . .) Chicago's home uniforms featured a white jersey with a flared-out blue collar, while the roadies had blue on blue. Both jerseys were worn with either white or blue trousers—or, in the summer of 1976, with no trousers at all.

On August 8, the White Sox took the field at home against the Kansas City Royals to open a doubleheader during a hot Chicago summer. Instead of their traditional nontraditional uniforms, the Sox were adorned in navy blue Bermuda-length shorts, white knee socks with two blue stripes at the top, and their usual pajama-style jerseys. It was a design by Veeck's wife, who obviously never intended for her husband's players to hear taunts like "You guys are the sweetest team we've seen" from the Royals' John Mayberry.

Besides being the biggest embarrassment for Chicago baseball since the 1919 World Series, the uniforms didn't serve a functional purpose. Players' legs were exposed, meaning it would be skin-on-dirt on any slide to a base. And who exactly is going to be diving for a ball in the outfield when he's guaranteed to leave the play with two bloody knees?

As was often the case with Veeck, serendipity ruled the day. Despite their "shorts-comings," the White Sox won the front end of the twin bill, 5–2. That didn't stop manager Paul Richards from changing his team into long pants for the nightcap, which, naturally, Chicago lost by the score of 7–1.

According to *SI*, the shorts reappeared for two other games that season before being stowed away in the deepest, darkest corners of Comiskey Park. Chicago would wear its pajama tops until 1982, when it moved to a red, white, and blue design with a large "SOX" across the chest. The team changed uniforms again in 1987, before settling on the black-and-white design in 1990 that became one of the most successful sports merchandising decisions of the decade.

Giving Steve Howe
an Eighth Chance

"She Don't Lie, She Don't Lie, She Don't Lie . . . Cocaine"

LEFT-HANDED pitching will always be at a premium in the major leagues. There's a reason why the finally retired Jesse Orosco is the only pitcher in baseball history to appear in 1,252 games while also having been present when man discovered fire.

Steve Howe happened to be a left-handed pitcher with a bit of talent. He had a great fastball and was the National League Rookie of the Year in 1980 after saving 17 games for the Los Angeles Dodgers. But he also had a raging cocaine addiction (that explains the fastballs) and checked into rehab after the 1982 season.

Howe returned to the Dodgers and opened the 1983 season with 14 straight relief appearances without giving up an earned run. But that streak ended in May, when Howe had a relapse and returned to drug rehab for a second time. In July, he was suspended by Los Angeles for two days for reporting late to a game. In September, Howe was suspended again by the Dodgers because he missed a team flight to Atlanta and refused to take a urinalysis drug test when he finally made it to Georgia. Although the Dodgers made the postseason, Howe was banned from participating in the National League Championship Series.

In December 1983, commissioner Bowie Kuhn suspended Howe and three other players without pay for the entire 1984 baseball season. Seems Howe had tested positive for cocaine during three separate voluntary examinations in November. Oops.

Howe returned to the Dodgers in 1985, but they released him later that season. He signed with Minnesota and pitched for the Twins for 13 games, but they, too, released him in September for what they called a "temporary recurrence" of his drug addiction. In 1986, Howe hooked up with San Jose of the California League (not to be confused with the California Penal League, home to fire-balling right-hander Ricky "Wild Thing" Vaughn). During the 1986 season, the National Association of Professional Baseball Leagues suspended Howe twice as he allegedly tested positive for cocaine. On December 31, San Jose dropped Howe from its roster.

In 1987, the Texas Rangers signed Steve Howe—now in his seventh year of drug addiction—to a two-year contract. In January 1988, he was released by Texas for violating his aftercare program with consumption of alcohol. (Wonder if that 4.31 ERA had any impact on the decision?) In November 1991, the New York Yankees signed Howe to a one-year contract. In December 1991, Howe was arrested for possession of cocaine in Montana. The following June, Howe pled guilty in U.S. district court to a misdemeanor charge of attempting to buy a gram of cocaine. Commissioner Fay Vincent decided to give Howe his seventh suspension and made this one stick—Howe became the first player in baseball history to receive a lifetime ban for drug policy violations. But in November 1992, arbitrator George Nicolau shortened

Howe's suspension to time served because he deduced that the pitcher's drug addiction stemmed from adult attention deficit disorder. (Why does this suddenly sound like an episode of *Maury*?)

Howe pitched for the Yankees from 1993 to 1996 and had a stellar 1994 season, with 15 saves and a 1.80 ERA. The Bombers, however, dumped Howe in June 1996 with his ERA at a not-so-stellar 6.35. Two days after his release, Howe was arrested at Kennedy International Airport for carrying a loaded gun in his luggage. He pled guilty and got off with three years of probation and community service.

Jeez . . . imagine if the batters Howe faced were allowed as many strikes as he was?

Aluminum Bats

Allowing College Middle Infielders to Hit .750 since 1970

*O*N OCCASION *in this book, it becomes imperative to share an extraordinary point of view on a given theme. The only way to truly accomplish that is by appointment of a guest essayist on said topic. This is one such instance.*

Hello down there. I'm *Fraxinus americana*. The white ash.

Yes, I'm one of God's botanical wonders. Not that it matters to any of you people. You think trees like me should just be sliced up, dried in a kiln, ground down on a lathe, and then wielded by some tobacco-chewing lunkhead to smack a ball over a wall.

As you probably guessed, I'm not a fan of baseball, just like I'm not a fan of lumberjacks, Dutch elm disease, or kids that climb on me after using the toilet. The sport lost its appeal several years ago when I saw Bo Jackson break a cousin of mine over his knee following a strikeout.

So I hate baseball. But boy, do I love aluminum bats!

Metal bats were popularized first by the Easton Company in the late 1970s. Everyone—weekend warriors, Little League tykes, college players—dropped their wood and grabbed some aluminum. Why? Because even that weird kid who's always forced to play right field (you know, the one who can't

Like their cave-dwelling brethren, aluminum bats also sleep upside down.
(Greg Wyshynski)

run without tripping on his own pants and is constantly picking his nose) will knock the damn cowhide off the ball with a metallic boom stick.

Besides sparing the lives of a forest's worth of my friends, the proliferation of aluminum bats has been satisfying on several fronts. For instance, pitchers in high school and college ball don't develop their mechanics like they used to because they pitch scared—it's hard to paint the corners when a ball near the hands on a metal bat can still travel 300 feet to centerfield. Hitters, meanwhile, go from pounding the ball on the amateur level to getting humbled in the minor leagues with a wooden bat. Wanna know why bunting in Major League Baseball is a lost art? Because players never have to lay one down when they're hitting .500 with a metal bat. It hurts the sport—any baseball fan will tell you that you can't spell "fun" without "fundamentals."

More good news for me at least: between 1991 and 2001, eight players were killed by batted balls from aluminum bats. At this rate, the ratio of humans to trees will be perfect for a massive agricultural uprising around 3010.

The bottom line is that aluminum bats have been really good to the tree, shrub, and twig community, but we still haven't been able to solve the root of the problem in the big leagues.

Will we ever find a way to get Major League Baseball players to lose their wood?

Chances are, they'll never make the switch. Do you know how hard it is to cork an aluminum bat?

San Francisco's Crazy Crab
A Claws for Concern by the Bay

PERHAPS IT'S a relief that the worst mascot in professional sports history was intended to be just that. But those who had to endure the Crazy Crab's only season may beg to differ.

By 1984, mascots in Major League Baseball were becoming commonplace at the stadium, led by San Diego's superlative Chicken. The San Francisco Giants decided they wanted in on the man-in-suit fun, so the team held a poll to find out what kind of mascot its fans desired to see at the ballpark. Two-thirds of respondents said they didn't want one at all. Perhaps inspired by this potential backlash, the Giants decided to unleash pro sports' first "antimascot." The Crazy Crab was born.

The Crab itself was about as endearing as a foul ball off the kneecap. It was constructed from cheap foam, had two wandering eyes, and resembled a mutant pancake stricken with agoraphobia. It was a mascot that only Andy Kauffman could love—one whose sole purpose was to draw the ire of the fans and players. A television commercial introduced the mascot by showing manager Frank Robinson having to be restrained from attacking it. Fans were encouraged to jeer the Crab. They booed and bombarded the mascot with various projectiles before, during, and after the game.

Crazy Crab fans rally to bring the hated mascot back at Crustacean Commotion, held July 9, 2005, in San Francisco. (Courtesy of Rehabthecrab.com)

According to the Giants' official website, the actor playing the Crazy Crab had a legitimate fear that a fan might fire a gun at him from the stands in the team's final home game of the season. No word if the Crab was equally panicky about a fan smuggling in a vat of melted butter.

The Giants' final game of the 1984 season was the Crazy Crab's final game as team mascot. Rumor has it that the Crab spent the rest of the decade fielding offers from high schools interested in having him lecture on the dangers of sexually transmitted diseases.

Nearly Every Thought That Escaped Charlie O. Finley's Head
He Put the "O" in "Crazy"

DID YOU ever hear something that made you want to take a bottle and smash it over your skull to make sure that you weren't dreaming and that you had actually heard what you thought you had just heard?

It happens to me—like, a lot. It happened the first time that I heard that Oakland A's owner Charlie O. Finley passed on a young pitching prospect named Don Sutton. Why did he pass on him? Because Sutton didn't have a nickname and wasn't interested in ever having one. So the man who christened Jim "Catfish" Hunter and John "Blue Moon" Odom let Sutton sign with the Los Angeles Dodgers, and 324 wins later the righty was inducted into the Hall of Fame.

Finley is one of the game's most complex characters. On the one hand, he was like baseball's version of Arthur C. Clarke: a futurist who helped establish traditions such as free agency, World Series night games, eye-catching uniforms, and interleague play. On the other hand, Finley was nuttier than George Washington Carver's kitchen and a much-loathed cheapskate to his championship-caliber players. Looking back at Finley's 18-year tenure as owner of the Kansas City/Oakland A's, the phrase "stranger than fiction" keeps running through your head like the crawl at the bottom of a 24-hour news channel. See if you can separate the fact from the fantasy; the fake stories are identified at the end of this quiz:

1. Finley advocated using orange baseballs, which batters could see more easily, increasing offensive output. (Let's see: orange baseballs with kelly green and gold uniforms? A's games would have had the same spectrum as the bathroom floor of a frat house on Sunday morning.)

2. Finley created an unofficial mascot for his teams: a mule that he paraded around the ballpark, through the press box, even into cocktail parties. Named Charlie O. (a jackass named after . . . well, you know), the mule was a big hit with the fans. Unfortunately, for any nonspectator at the ballpark, the mule also had an incontinence problem. Let's just say the Kansas City A's weren't the only crappy product on the field during the 1960s.

3. He advocated making three balls, rather than four, a walk. His argument was that basketball is 5-on-5 and football is 11-on-11 but baseball is 9-against-1. "We've got to give the batter help," Finley was quoted as saying. Genius . . .

4. Municipal Stadium in Kansas City didn't just have a home plate. It had THE HOME PLATE OF THE FUTURE™: a compressed air device installed below the plate that blew dirt away. Should the umpire run out of baseballs, no need to call over the batboy—a mechanical rabbit named "Harvey," dressed in an A's jersey, would pop out of the ground to deliver new balls when the umpire pressed a button with his foot.

5. Finley advocated installing a 20-second "pitch clock" to enforce baseball's rule that a pitcher must throw the ball 20 seconds after receiving it from the catcher. Finley argued that some pitchers "throw once every half hour." Obviously, he never saw Phil Niekro play; a half hour was generous . . .

6. In 1974, Finley made 11-year-old batboy Stanley Burrell honorary vice president of the A's. Burrell used his baseball moxie to embark on a music career, eventually taking up the moniker M. C. Hammer and selling millions of records by sampling an old Rick James song about freaky girls.

7. Among the gimmicks that Finley used to lure fans to the ballpark were Bald-Head Night, in which follicly challenged fans got half-priced tickets; Mustache Day, in which the follicly blessed received free admission; Farmer's Night, complete with pregame pig chases; and Hot-Pants Day, where ladies wearing the sexy duds were given free admission and permitted to participate in a pregame fashion-show parade. Although Finley's stunts were reminiscent of master showman Bill Veeck's, Veeck was once quoted as saying that "Charlie Finley does things without class."

ANSWERS: *Actually, there isn't a fake story among them. You couldn't make this stuff up if you tried . . .*

MORONIC MEDIA

TV Timeouts
We'll Be Back in a Moment

MY FATHER and I were at a New York Jets game some years ago, huddled under a large transparent plastic poncho as we attempted to avoid a downpour of rain in the upper deck. I remember suddenly feeling a slight tug on my jersey through the synthetic blanket. I turned to my left and saw a man sitting next to me, soaking wet, tugging again. "Heeeey . . . hey kid," he croaked in a voice so slurred that one could safely assume he'd been tailgating since the end of last season. He tugged my arm again, and I raised the poncho to find out what was up. "You see . . . You see the guy down there?" asked my inebriated new friend, his words conjoined like Siamese triplets. "The guy with the orange arm . . . the orange arm down there?"

I peered down at the sideline. Sure enough, a man was standing not far from the bench, raising his arm in the air, as orange as a glass of Tropicana. Curiously, there was no action on the field, yet neither team had called a timeout. So I said to the guy, "What's his deal?" And Hiccup McBoozehound replied, quite cogently, "When that guy's arm is up, it means TV timeout. When his arm is down, then they play football again."

I don't know why this gentleman chose to impart this information onto me. But ever since then, I've not only paid attention to the sideline TV coordinator at football games but also fearlessly engaged the drunks sitting next to me in open dialogue about life and love.

TV timeouts, by the way, are an affront to anyone who's ever paid to watch a live sporting event. Timeouts aren't just a chance for veteran players to grab their oxygen; they're tactical measures used by opposing coaches to change the momentum of a game. That's why you only get a finite number of them in basketball and football. In hockey, you get one. That's how important it is. But because of television, teams get an extra set of timeouts at predetermined points within the game. Coaches game-plan around them. Fans in the arena and the stadium are left watching disjointed play and long pointless breaks in the action. All of this would, of course, seem worthy if the revenue they generated translated into lower ticket and concession prices. Yeah, when Tony Siragusa flies!

TV timeouts actually negatively affect game play. Lou Lamoriello, president of the NHL's New Jersey Devils, said in a 2004 radio interview with WFAN in New York that TV timeouts are a big reason why goal scoring had plummeted in the league. He said that defensive players simply get too much rest during a televised game, much more than that in the precable-dominated days of the early 1980s, when the Gretzkys and Bossys of the world were scoring over 60 goals a season. Players today simply don't get a healthy dose of fatigue; no wonder most playoff games go into four overtimes.

The powers-that-be know that all of these stoppages in play, each for three minutes of commercials, are bad for the flow of the game and are an insult to the paying customers. We know how awful they feel by the manner in which they attempt to compensate for the breaks during basketball and football games: by bribing us with squads of gyrating cheerleaders.

Any time you see a gaggle of blondes doing a floor routine to "Rump Shaker," you know that someone's trying to distract your ass from something pretty heinous . . .

Brian Dennehy Does the "General"

ESPN Has a Bad Knight

SPORTS MOVIES have seen more dramatic miscastings than the one featured here—John Turturro's turn as Howard Cosell in *Monday Night Mayhem* leaps to mind. But big, burly Brian Dennehy as former Indiana Hoosiers coach Bobby Knight in ESPN's 2002 made-for-TV flick *A Season on the Brink?* Ladies and gentlemen, the tale of the tape.

	Robert "Bobby" Montgomery Knight	Brian Dennehy
Nickname	"The General"	"That Guy from *Cocoon*"
Occupation	Collegiate men's basketball coach	Master thespian
Born	October 25, 1940, Massillon, Ohio	July 9, 1938, Bridgeport, Connecticut
Education	Ohio State University	Columbia University

	Robert "Bobby" Montgomery Knight	Brian Dennehy
Professional debut	Assistant coach, Cuyahoga Falls High School, Ohio (1962)	"Peter Connor" in *Kojak*, episode 4.15 (1973)
Military background	Coached at West Point for six seasons	Served in United States Marine Corps
Combined NCAA national titles won as coach and player	Four	Zero
Combined appearances on *Dynasty* and *Just Shoot Me*	Zero	Nine
Appeared in *A Season on the Brink*	1986	2003
Quotation that will set him off into a violent rage	"Hey, what's up, Knight?" —Kent Harvey, Indiana freshman	"You're lucky to be breathing." —Colonel Samuel Trautman, *First Blood*
Most disgusting moment	Allegedly shows players a soiled piece of toilet paper for motivation	In *Gladiator* (1992), wears a black Lycra bodysuit in movie-ending boxing match

GLOW PUCKS AND 10-CENT BEER

	Robert "Bobby" Montgomery Knight	Brian Dennehy
Famous choke	Neil Reed, 1997	*Birdland* (1994), canceled in its first season
Monster moment	Allegedly threw a vase near Indiana athletic-department secretary Jeanette Hartgraves	Played John Wayne Gacy in *To Catch a Killer* (1992)
The media says . . .	"Bobby admits he has 'a temper problem'— which is like Jeffrey Dahmer saying that he suffers from an eating disorder." —*Time*, May 17, 2000	"Dennehy has a powerful performance, hampered only by the fact that he doesn't look or sound a whole lot like Knight." —*St. Louis Post-Dispatch*, March 9, 2002
Heard cursing on basic cable?	Yes	Yes
Resemblance to Bobby Knight?	Looks just like him	Uh, sure . . . if Bobby Knight spent a few years at the buffet maybe . . .

The *Heidi* Game
A Decision as Cold as the Alps

HOW APPROPRIATE that Jennifer Edwards, who played that adorable little goatherder in 1968's made-for-TV version of *Heidi*, also appeared in a film called *A Fine Mess*.

On November 17, 1968, the New York Jets traveled to Oakland to face the Raiders in a highly anticipated game between two star-studded teams, boasting names such as Joe Namath, Daryle Lamonica, and Fred Biletnikoff. Both AFL teams were 7–2 on the season and had established a brutal cross-country rivalry over the years.

The game was a penalty-filled thriller, featuring no fewer than five lead changes and a four-touchdown performance from Lamonica. It all came down to a sensational climax in the fourth quarter, as Jim Turner kicked a 26-yard field goal to give the Jets a 32–29 lead.

If only that had been the climax.

With one minute, five seconds left in the game, the Raiders had plenty of time to strike back, and strike they did: halfback Charlie Smith caught a 43-yard touchdown pass from Lamonica for a 36–32 lead. On the kickoff back to the Jets—who still had 42 seconds left for a final drive—Oakland fullback

Preston Ridlehuber scooped up a loose ball and ran it in for another Raiders touchdown, making it 43–32 for the home team.

The Oakland victory would be news to viewers in the Eastern and Central time zones because, after watching over three and a half quarters of football, they didn't get to see the game end.

Since the telecast had run past 7:00 PM Eastern time, NBC switched viewers to *Heidi* during the commercial break following Turner's field goal. Instead of two dramatic touchdowns in a crucial regular-season game, fans were treated to two hours of Jean Simmons as Fräulein Rottenmeier.

The decision came down to money. NBC had sold advertising time during the film to Timex and had to show the movie in the 7:00 PM–9:00 PM time frame to fill that obligation. So even though those players were still taking a licking, to its broadcasting plan NBC was sticking.

Angry fans flooded NBC's phone lines, infuriated they weren't shown the end of the game. (The calls actually began during the fourth quarter in anticipation that the network would cut away.) The excruciating bungle made the front page of the *New York Times* the following day, and NBC president Julian Goodman issued a formal apology.

You can judge how horrendous an error in judgment is by how sweeping the measures are to correct it. In the case of the *Heidi* game, networks began scheduling television programs around sporting events and not vice versa. It began an era of "sliding" start times rather than "already in progress" cut-ins.

Subjective Lists about Sports
Hey! Who Put This on the List?

*O*N OCCASION *in this book, it becomes imperative to share an extraordinary point of view on a given theme. The only way to truly accomplish that is through the appointment of a guest essayist on said topic. This is one such instance.*

Hi . . . I'm this author's Objectivity. Perhaps you've met my cousin Subjectivity a few times during the course of this book. The initial agreement was that we'd have an equal participation in creating a list of the 101 worst ideas in sports history, but after reading that rant about the Deion Sanders album, I'm pretty sure the deal's off.

Lists, sportscentric or otherwise, should offer a balance between objective and subjective thought—along with some heaping spoonfuls of common sense. It's that last part that ESPN had trouble with when compiling its list of the greatest North American athletes of the 20th century. Michael Jordan topped the list, followed by Babe Ruth, Muhammad Ali, Jim Brown, Wayne Gretzky, and Jesse Owens. Not bad, right? One can objectively look at their achievements, their individual legacies in their respective sports, what it takes for human beings to excel in these sports, and take an informed measurement of their "greatness."

Notice that I specify "human beings." I did so because ESPN decided to list not one, not two, but *three* equine "athletes" on its list of the top 100. There was Secretariat at No. 35, ahead of Mickey Mantle (37), Lawrence Taylor (40), and Mario Lemieux (55). There was Man O'War (84), who ranked higher than Otto Graham (86) and Bob Beamon (91). And there was Citation (97), who ranked ahead of Don Budge, Sam Snead, Jack Johnson, and about a million other men and women left off the list.

There's no question that these three racehorses are the best in the 20th century . . . at being racehorses. As athletes, they're no better than Gretzky's stick or A. J. Foyt's car; they're accessories utilized by real athletes. Even if you want to characterize them as "athletes," there's no objective way to compare their achievements with those of human beings. It'd be like having Jack Nicholson competing for Best Actor against Lassie.

Would Citation have won the Triple Crown without a rider, or did Eddie Arcaro (No. 66 on the ESPN list) have a little something to do with that success? And don't give me that "symbiotic relationship" business. Yes, a jockey needs a horse like a horse needs a jockey. But that sure as hell doesn't make Secretariat a better athlete than Mickey Mantle. (Mr. Ed, on the other hand, not only hit a home run at Dodger Stadium but could also hold a conversation . . . depending on the amount of nylon mesh put under his top lip.)

In 1996, the NBA revealed its triumph of senseless subjectivity: the 50 greatest players of the league's first 50 years. (Of the 50 voters who compiled the team, 22 were actually players on the completed list; how's that for fair and balanced?) The list, like any list, is a powder keg of subjective debate. (Patrick Ewing instead of Bob Lanier? Scottie Pippen over . . . well, anyone?) But the panel's real crime was its overwhelming disregard for players who built the foundation of the league, such as Joe Fulks, one of the NBA's first leading scorers and an innovator of the jump shot. Fulks was good enough to make the NBA's 25-man Silver Anniversary team in 1971. Are you telling me that in the next 25 years, there were 26 players better than he was in the NBA?

But that's subjectivity for you. They should call it *suck-jectivity*. Hey . . . I'm just being objective here.

Miller, Fouts Join
Monday Night Football

"Like the Eagles munching on Prometheus's liver at Mount Caucasus, babe . . ."

ONE OF THE worst disasters in the history of sports television could only be born of great potential. In 1999, Dan Dierdorf parted ways with *Monday Night Football*, leaving former NFL quarterback Boomer Esiason and play-by-play veteran Al Michaels in the booth. What appeared to be addition by subtraction turned out to be a recipe for disaster: Michaels and Boomer seemed about as comfortable as a first date in an airport bar.

Esiason left *MNF* after the season, with the ratings in a nosedive. Executive producer Don Ohlmeyer—who had a hand in the show's success during its Howard Cosell–starring glory years—promised a major overhaul. In June 2000, he announced the addition of college football analyst (and ex-NFL quarterback) Dan Fouts and comedian Dennis Miller to the *MNF* team.

Miller had become, in the years following his stint doing "Weekend Update" on *Saturday Night Live*, one of the top political humorists in the country on his HBO talk show and as a stand-up comedian. He beat out conservative radio host Rush Limbaugh for the *MNF* job, depriving us—for three years—of Rush's views on how the media protects and coddles black quarterbacks. Ohlmeyer clearly saw this as an updated version of the greatest *MNF* team of all time, with Michaels as Keith Jackson, Fouts as Don Meredith, and Miller as a more controllable Cosell. "I think, with this trio, we'll provide a telecast that will be relevant to football experts, accessible to occasional fans and unpredictable for both," Ohlmeyer told the press.

What turned out to be unpredictable was how immensely the Michaels-Fouts-Miller team would flop. Miller—while a brilliant comedian in his element—was as well suited for a primetime football broadcast as Carrot Top would have been discussing the socioeconomic landscape of Senegal on *Face the Nation*.

There were two problems with Miller. First, Ohlmeyer didn't want Miller's political humor to alienate any viewers, so he ordered it kept to a minimum, which is like telling Tom Jones to sing soprano. It also didn't help that Miller really didn't know all that much about football to begin with.

Second, because *MNF* is on ABC, Miller couldn't use the colorful language that he masterfully applied on cable television. To paraphrase Jean Shepherd from *A Christmas Story*, Miller used obscenities "like some artists used oil or clay. It was his true medium."

One could say that Miller was also too smart for the room. But how smart could he have been not to know—before taking the job—that Sylvia Plath references wouldn't fly with an audience that still giggles at the name Marion Butts?

So Miller was a bust. But at least you noticed that he was there, unlike the pseudoanalytical nothing whom we Earthlings called Dan Fouts. He was invisible, every game. Sure, you'd hear a low rumble now and again ("hmmmmmm . . . Chargers . . . hmmmmmmmm"), but Fouts never increased his decibels over mouse-fart levels at any point in the season.

The most accurate measure of this catastrophe was Al Michaels's performance during the Miller-Fouts run in the booth. He was awful, but could you blame him? How hard must it have been to spout off another "Do you believe in miracles?" line when you're stuck in a room with a mute on your right and a guy on your left comparing Bill Walsh to Vladimir Kosma Zworykin (inventor of the kinescope, for the Miller impaired).

Ratings continued to fall, viewers hated the booth, and in 2002 the Miller-Fouts era came to an unceremonious end. John Madden, the best color commentator in the business, was hired away from FOX to join Michaels. Ratings began to rebound the next season.

Pay-Per-View Boxing
A Bigger Mess Than Don King's Hair after Skydiving

THE FOLLOWING is the actual shooting script from the Derrick "Death Blow" Jackson/Tony "Bone Adjuster" Smith fight for the International Championship Universal Pugilism title in 2002.

9:00 PM EST: Announcers greet the pay-per-viewers, who have dropped $49.99 to watch this historic battle between modern-day gladiators.

9:01–10:00 PM: The announcers discuss why this fight is considered a historic battle between modern-day gladiators. Video vignettes tell the story of how these two modern-day gladiators arrived in this historic battle.

10:01 PM: A seven-minute montage is shown of upcoming battles between modern-day gladiators that can be purchased for $49.99 a pop.

10:08–10:35 PM: Further discussion of why this fight is considered a historic battle between modern-day gladiators, this time with colorful bar graphs and pie charts just like those in *USA Today*.

10:36–10:49 PM: A hyperactive little leprechaun named Harold Something-or-other speaks at ring side about punch stats, Marquis of Queensbury rules, and other technicalities that the casual viewer couldn't give two bites on Holyfield's ear about.

10:50–11:47 PM: Even more discussion, even more video vignettes, then some more discussion, and then a shot of some Z-list celebrities in the crowd, followed by painstakingly lengthy polemic on why this fight is considered a historic battle between modern-day gladiators.

11:48 PM: Some guy with a bad tan and a rented tux steps to the middle of the ring to do the umpteenth version of a copyrighted announcing catchphrase (*Let's get ready to grummmmmble!*).

11:58 PM: After the referee, judges, timekeepers, ring-card girls, beer sponsors, promoters, corner men, medics, Donald Trump, and the announcer's mother-in-law are introduced, Smith and Jackson make their way to the ring via incomprehensible hip-hop entrance music and in hideous sequined robes that look like they were rescued from Jackie Stallone's goodwill donation pile.

12:07 AM: The fighters are given instructions, touch gloves, and come out fighting.

12:07:45 AM: Jackson knocks out Smith to defend the ICUP heavyweight championship.

12:08–12:15 AM: The announcers briefly touch on what a historic battle between modern-day gladiators the fight was; Jackson babbles about being the greatest butterfly that ever stung like a bee; and the broadcast ends with three minutes of technical staff credits.

This scenario exists three out of every four times there's an overhyped pay-per-view boxing match. Paying $50 for 120 minutes of teasing and then 40 seconds of action makes this the biggest rip-off since the invention of 1-900 phone sex lines.

But that's a pinprick compared with the damage that pay-per-view has inflicted on the sport of boxing itself. Toward the end of the 20th century, the sweet science degenerated from an American athletic institution to a cult sport that didn't garner the ratings to warrant network television exposure. Much like its ugly stepcousin professional wrestling, it found a home on cable TV and pay-per-view broadcasts. When there was a legitimate draw—for Tyson, De la Hoya, Roy Jones Jr., or even Big George Foreman—boxing had every bit the cultural impact as it had in its glory years. But pay-per-view quickly destroyed boxing's star system. Former champions hung on years beyond the sunset of their prime for a taste of PPV dollars. Mediocre boxers were hyped into title contenders by promoters desperate for big-money matchups. These Glass Joes were quickly exposed, but that didn't stop promoters from recycling them several more times, sometimes against the same opponents who had already demolished them. The heavyweight division soon became the boxing equivalent of a traveling home-run derby populated by two dozen Pete Incaviglias.

Pay-per-view's most putrid pustules on professional boxing are at its most basic level of sports fanaticism. Does it make a lick of sense to take a sport with limited appeal and a diminishing fan base and then force people to pay to see fights that HBO wouldn't bump its 27th monthly showing of *X-Men* for?

Pay-per-view all but knocked boxing out of the mainstream.

SHANKS, DUFFS, AND SLICES

PART 4

Fantasy Golf

The Fantasy? That It Isn't Insipid and Tedious

I 'M ALL about fantasy sports and a bit of a snob about them. I'll only enter hockey groups that score penalty minutes and shorthanded assists. You want to start five wide receivers every Sunday? Then you don't want me in your football league. During most summer mornings, I've set my pitching rotation before I've brushed my teeth. My impudence naturally causes me to loathe fantasy golf and auto racing. Both games defy the most basic tenets of fantasy sporting, which is the spirit of competition. In other fantasy sports, you're either battling team managers for a specific pool of players, or there are financial restrictions in place (in rotisserie-style leagues) that ensure that managers aren't simply populating their teams with the best players in the game. In most golf and auto-racing fantasy leagues, you can have Tiger Woods or the winner of the Daytona 500 on your team without a single repercussion for the rest of your lineup or to the rest of the teams in your league. You're basically George Steinbrenner, minus the luxury tax, able to gobble up the best and the brightest without recourse.

The rules for both games are really lame, too. Most leagues split golfers or drivers into three talent pools. You must set your lineup based on those three levels each week. This is all kinds of stupid, because if every team in the league chooses the top two from Pool A and the top three from Pool B, then all of a sudden it's a bunch of Pool-C-ers—marginal talents who miss the cut every week—deciding a league champion. It's like a fantasy baseball league in which the team with the best backup catcher wins.

The other huge flaws in these fantasy games are the limitations of player usage. For example, if you have Tiger Woods on your squad, you can only use him in a maximum number of tournaments (typically 10) before he can no longer score points for you. Are golf and racing so intrinsically predictable that simply having the "best" players guarantees victory? What about margin of error? Imagine a fantasy hockey league in which the NHL's top goalie could only appear in half the games. What a joke!

So why, ultimately, is fantasy golf a worse idea than fantasy auto racing? Because, at some point, you might have to drop a racer from your roster because he died when his car slammed into a wall at 160 miles per hour.

Say what you will about the validity of NASCAR as a sport, but that is hardcore . . .

Regulating Golf Courses, Not Equipment

Diff'rent Strokes Rule Their World, Yes They Do . . .

THERE'S A great scene in that white-guy-goes-nutso flick *Falling Down* in which Michael Douglas's character refers to a luxurious private golf course as a place where acres of park land have been hijacked for a "bunch of old men driving around in little cars." (Then, of course, he scares a man into cardiac arrest by brandishing a shotgun and delivering last rites that include an observation that the man will die wearing a stupid "golf hat.")

Maybe Kirk's son wouldn't have been so acrimonious if golf courses weren't so damn gluttonous about their real estate. But who can blame them? With practically no uniform equipment standards, country clubs need fairways the size of Route 66 just to keep things interesting these days.

Advancements in club technology have made nearly every golfer a better driver than their predecessors. The average driving distance on the PGA Tour increased from 275 yards to just under 300 from 1992 to 2002. In response to that growth, Augusta National added 300 yards in length to its Masters course in 2002.

71

Golf equipment, like these drivers, needs regulation. (Greg Wyshynski)

As with clubs, the PGA does not enforce the use of standardized golf balls. Every player can play his own. Imagine if a baseball hitter, after grabbing his personalized bat, got to select his own baseball to have pitched to him? "No, not that one . . . the one that bounces like a Super Happy Fun Ball, *por favor.*"

Look, I'm no Chi-Chi Trevino when it comes to golf, so I defer to the experts. Jack Nicklaus, for one, argued for years that every player should use the same type of ball and that the balls should be made less lively by either lowering compression or making the ball lighter. Pro golfers can still use their NASA-designed drivers and clubs, but the individual skill of the players—not simply the qualities of the ball they hit—will determine success. Combine that with a near compliance in standards between rule-making bodies in the United States Golf Association and the Royal and Ancient Golf Club of St. Andrews and soon clubs could be more uniform as well.

So what's standing in the way of a simple solution to this course-altering problem? More like who is standing in the way: Titleist, Nike, Callaway, Pinnacle, Top-Flite, and Wilson, for starters.

The PGA would get sued by every major equipment company whose balls are no longer used on the tour or whose equipment didn't meet newly stringent restrictions. Not to mention lawsuits by players whose endorsement dollars dry up the minute that the PGA creates uniformity in its gear guidelines.

Boy, sounds like the PGA's sponsors have the tour by the . . . uh . . . standardized equipment.

The Battle at Bighorn
What's Worse Than Bad Golf?
Exhibition Bad Golf!

IN 1999, golf fans made time in their leisurely paced schedules to watch Tiger Woods do just about anything: Play in a meaningless minor tournament. Sell a Buick. Read the phone book. Wash his balls.

Naturally, this obsession led to an exhibition golf sideshow called *Showdown at Sherwood*. This overhyped event—ABC's own *Monday Night Golf*–like summer broadcasting creation—featured Tiger taking on rival and the PGA's No. 2–ranked golfer David Duval in a million-dollar match-play event at Sherwood Country Club in Thousand Oaks, California. The "showdown" had all the drama of watching your grandparents play Parcheesi, but it garnered an impressive 6.9 rating for ABC.

That led to a second exhibition, 2000's *Battle at Bighorn*, between Woods and Sergio Garcia at Bighorn Country Club in Palm Desert, California. This one was a bit better, as Garcia clearly relished the role as Tiger's foil and in fact defeated Woods in the event—one that drew an impressive 7.6 rating for the network.

In 2001, Tiger suggested that the format should change (gee . . . wonder why?). That summer, ABC presented a cross-gender *Battle at Bighorn* team-up between Tiger and LPGA star Annika Sorenstam against Duval and LPGA champ Karrie Webb. And boy, what battles they were: between the golfers and the fast greens, the golfers and a stiff desert wind, and the LPGA golfers and their institutional putting deficiencies.

Woods and Duval both drove the ball like weekend duffers. Webb sent a 20-foot putt 40 feet past the hole, while Sorenstam sent her own 20-foot chance nearly 70 feet long. All of the players spent more time in the bunkers than soldiers on Iwo Jima did in 1945. The event limped to an overtime finish, with Tiger and Annika screwing up the least to split $1.2 million. The 6.1 million people who tuned in were not, as of this writing, offered a refund on their electric bills.

The disastrous event sent ABC's golf exhibition franchise into a tailspin. The following year's *Battle at Bighorn*, between teams of Tiger/Jack Nicklaus versus Garcia/Lee Trevino, produced a 5.1 rating. In 2003, the *Battle at the Bridges* in Rancho Santa Fe, California, between teams of Woods/Ernie Els and Garcia/Phil Mickelson, garnered just a 4.6 rating, down 10 percent from the previous year. In 2004, the second *Battle at the Bridges*, with Woods and Hank Kuehne taking on Mickelson and John Daly, sunk to a 3.6 rating—a 55 percent drop from the Woods/Garcia match in 2000. The lackluster ratings had Woods's agents claiming that ABC didn't give the "battle" enough promotional support.

Wasn't putting an exhibition golf event on in prime time promotion enough?

The *Battle at the Bridges* returned in 2005 with Woods/John Daly against Mickelson/Retief Goosen, but Tiger's reps said it would be his last *Monday Night Golf* event for the foreseeable future. The match drew a 3.9 rating.

STADI-DUMBS

PART 5

RANK No. 96

The Retirement of Nos. 42 and 99

Baseball and Hockey Make a Numerical Blunder

WHEN WAYNE Gretzky was 10 years old, he wore No. 9 for his Novice A team in honor of his idol, Gordie Howe, and scored 378 goals in 85 games. In 20 seasons in the National Hockey League, again honoring Howe by wearing No. 99, he scored 894 goals on four different teams. But what if some young player, who busted his tail for hours every day skating on a backyard pond in some Canadian cow town, wanted to honor Gretzky by wearing No. 99 when he finally achieved his dream and skated in the NHL? No dice, canucklehead. In 2000, the NHL made Gretzky the only player in the history of the league to have his jersey retired by all of its teams. It followed the lead of Major League Baseball, which forced all of its franchises to retire Jackie Robinson's No. 42 in 1997.

There's no denying the impact that either athlete had on his respective sport, just like there's no denying the influence that they had on generations of aspiring athletes. So would there be any better way to honor Gretzky and

Robinson than to have the players they encouraged to pick up a stick or bat wear No. 99 or No. 42?

Twenty years from now, what would mean more to Jackie Robinson's legacy: to have No. 42 hang among dozens of honored digits on the outfield wall or to have the day's most prominent African American baseball player explain how Robinson influenced him to the point where he adopted the number as his own? In Gretzky's case, here's an interesting query: if he broke the majority of the NHL records set by his idol, Mr. Howe, shouldn't Gordie's number be officially put into mothballs as well as Wayne's?

Retiring numbers has become a bit of a farce over the years. Before the Florida Marlins even played their inaugural game, the team had retired No. 5 in honor of late team president Carl Barger's favorite player, Joe DiMaggio. (Strangely, the Yankees opted not to retire Florida infielder Orestes Destrade's No. 39 before opening day.)

Still, let's not forget the most heinous result of retiring the numbers of Wayne Gretzky and Jackie Robinson: the Calgary Flames were forced to retire the uniform number of the greatest Edmonton Oiler, and the San Francisco Giants were forced to retire the number of a legendary Los Angeles Dodger.

Blasphemy!

Warm-Weather Super Bowls
Meteorological Class Warfare

WHEN BART Starr returned to the huddle with 16 seconds remaining in Green Bay's December 31, 1967, NFL championship game against visiting Dallas, the temperature at Lambeau Field had dipped to 18 degrees below zero, Fahrenheit. The wind chill brought it all the way down to about 46 below. The field was frozen solid, a sheet of ice. Starr—bruised, battered leader of the Pack—called his own number, had center Ken Bowman and guard Jerry Kramer take out Cowboys lineman Jethro Pugh, and dove over the goal line for the winning touchdown. About 50,000 football fans braved the unbearably frosty conditions to watch the 21–17 classic that would forever be known as the Ice Bowl.

The game was in stark contrast to the Packers' Super Bowl II victory against Oakland—a game played in the balmy environs of Miami's Orange Bowl, where the only ice found was floating in club-level Mai Tais.

The NFL requires that the Super Bowl be played only in open-air stadiums located in cities with an average annual temperature of 50 degrees or higher on game day. Cities that average chillier temps must have a domed stadium to host the biggest moneymaking event in American professional sports. This rule is just completely asinine, for three reasons:

1. The NFL regular season isn't played in a vacuum. Teams such as Green Bay, Kansas City, Denver, Chicago, New York (Jets and Giants), New England, Pittsburgh, and Philadelphia all play in open-air stadiums that are at the mercy of the elements every fall and winter. That's at least 72 games that could, at any time, be played in ghastly weather conditions or plummeting temperatures. If teams have to overcome these challenges just to get to the Super Bowl, why don't they face them in the biggest game of the year? The second-most important games of the year—the AFC and NFC title contests—aren't shuttled off to some neutral site where the sun shines or the dome shields. Shouldn't the most important game meet the same standards?

2. It punishes fans in cold-weather cities. Can you imagine a league so egomaniacal that it thinks that it never has to hold its most significant annual event in New York, Chicago, Philadelphia, or Washington, D.C.? And what about the fans in Green Bay and Kansas City, who are undoubtedly some of the most dedicated in the entirety of sports? Don't they deserve a Super Bowl in their backyard more than, say, Falcons fans, who have now seen two?

3. It places celebrity above competition. The fact is that the NFL wants the Super Bowl to remain a social engagement for its celebrity fans and a weeklong kickback to its valued advertisers—none of whom can apparently shell out for a parka.

I wonder how many sitcom stars, R&B singers, and soft drink executives would have shown up to the Ice Bowl?

Variable Pricing
As If a $9 Beer Wasn't Enough of a Rip-Off

SAY YOU'RE a hockey fan, and one night you decide to see your hometown team play one of the NHL's elite. You saunter up to the arena and locate your usual ticket guy . . . only to find that the price of a seat has increased 20 percent because a popular opponent is in town. Fans commonly refer to this exercise as "ticket scalping"; the NHL and other major sports have another term for it, "variable pricing."

In 2002, three NHL teams began using the pricing method, sometimes referred to as "opponent pricing." Vancouver increased its single-game ticket prices by 20 percent for the Toronto Maple Leafs' two visits and 10 percent when Colorado, Detroit, and the New York Rangers came to town. Ottawa, another "small market" Canadian franchise, upped its tickets by 20 percent for the Maple Leafs and Red Wings. The Pittsburgh Penguins charged $5 more for several games featuring regional rivals. Two years later, Buffalo was the latest team to add variable pricing to its ticket plans.

In Major League Baseball, teams are using variable pricing based not only on opponents but on scheduling. The Chicago Cubs added between $3 and $10 per ticket for games played between June and August, as did the Toronto Blue Jays. Tampa Bay offered a more traditional pricing plan, gouging fans for home games against New York, Boston, and the San Francisco Giants, no matter when they were played.

Variable pricing is nothing new. European soccer teams have used opponent pricing against popular opponents for years. The University of Colorado has charged more for football home games against Oklahoma and Nebraska than for others. The University of Miami and Stanford University have done the same for their local rivalry games. Other comparisons abound, such as when concert venues charge more for the Rolling Stones than for the flavor-of-the-month pop band.

The noblest argument that the franchises have made is that most of the extra money raised in these "variable pricing" games will be from the fans visiting the arena to root for the road team. Indeed, it's hard to not like a plan in which Red Wings fans help Vancouver hang on to its free agents. But variable pricing is yet another exercise in screwing the average fan. Season-ticket holders and multiple-game package buyers are typically exempt from the markups, meaning that fans who can't afford such luxuries are penalized financially.

Where does this price gouging stop, exactly? Will every playoff team be grouped into "variable pricing" categories? Will fans pay different prices for every game depending on last year's standings? Consider this: some movie theaters are already charging slightly more for overhyped summer movies than for other films. At what point does variable pricing begin to alter the perception of consumers, who begin thinking that the lower-priced films aren't worth their time?

And isn't the real problem that the movie costs $10 to begin with and that a hockey ticket costs upwards of $28 for the cheap seats?

Grass in the Astrodome
Like Building a Farm in a Broom Closet

JUDGE ROY Hofheinz was a longtime booster of Houston-area sports. In the 1950s, he began banging the drum for a domed stadium in the city for the purposes of attracting a Major League Baseball team. In 1960, Houston was awarded an expansion franchise; two years later, construction began on what was then called the Harris County Domed Stadium. On April 9, 1965, the first major league game was played in the Astrodome between Houston and the New York Yankees. Even though the field was shielded from the sky by an enormous roof, the game was played on grass.

Hofheinz and the Astros thought that they had it all figured out when it came to playing baseball indoors: simply have grass developed that could grow in a temperature-controlled environment with slightly less-than-ideal sunlight. According to the *Rocky Mountain News*, that task fell to the agronomists from the University of Texas A&M. They developed a hybrid of Bermuda grass that they believed could survive on an indoor baseball field. The Lucite roof of the dome would act like a greenhouse, while the stadium's air conditioning would maintain the right amount of humidity.

Houston: You had a problem. To keep the grass alive, sunlight had to be let in through the dome. But during day games, the glare produced by the dome made it uncomfortable for fans and made fly balls become *Mission: Uncatchable* for infielders. So rather than risk having 18 players leave the field with massive head wounds every night, Astrodome officials decided to paint the roof.

As a result, grass that was already hard and dry—thanks to the dehydrating effects of the dome's air conditioning—wasn't getting but a fraction of the sunlight it needed to survive. When the color of the field began to fade, Astrodome officials again went the Sherwin Williams route, lathering the grass with green paint in order to mask its paltry appearance.

It didn't work. The 1966 season began sans the great grass experiment. (How the hell was that never the title for a Cheech and Chong movie?) In its place was something called Chemgrass . . . which you'll learn more about in a few chapters.

Personal Seat Licenses
The Frivolous Expenditure So Nice, You Pay for It Twice!

PERSONAL SEAT licenses are one-time fees that guarantee fans the opportunity to purchase a particular seat in their team's stadium on a seasonal basis for the rest of their lives. How does this differ from regular old run-of-the-mill, garden-variety season tickets, which guarantee fans the opportunity to purchase a particular seat in their team's stadium on a seasonal basis for the rest of their lives? Silly rabbit: PSLs give people who want to buy season tickets the opportunity to pay for the right to buy season tickets. Duh!

Why don't idiotic concepts like PSLs exist in other entertainment mediums? Couldn't you convince a bookworm that he needed to pay $5,000 just to reserve the right to purchase a copy when *Harry Potter and the Piggy Bank of Covetousness* comes out? Maybe the reason is that other forms of entertainment don't have enterprising charlatans such as Max Muhleman. Think of him as the Harold Hill of fan marketing: instead of trumpeting 76 trombones to the rubes, he ballyhooed 50,000 PSLs.

Muhleman, a former sportswriter who transitioned into public relations in the 1960s, first implemented the PSL plan for the expansion Charlotte

Hornets of the NBA in 1986. Then called permanent seat licenses, they were marketed to fans as a way to secure ownership of their own seats as well as the right to transfer the ticket to another party outside of their immediate family. At first, PSLs were free, but during the team's inaugural season, Muhleman began to see PSLs being offered on the open market for $5,000 apiece.

When Charlotte was being considered for an NFL franchise in 1993, Muhleman showed that he had learned his lesson. Working with team owner Jerry Richardson, the expansion Carolina Panthers charged between $600 and $5,400 per ticket for PSLs, telling fans that the capital they raised for a privately funded stadium could determine whether or not the city was awarded a team. Steve Rushin of *Sports Illustrated* summed up the madness nicely: "It is not clear if Richardson is required by North Carolina state law to carry a license to steal. Nor is it clear why, exactly, a license is necessary to buy a seat at a football game, especially when you consider that the NFL already has a seven-day waiting period between games."

Panthers fans broke open their commemorative Dale Earnhardt No. 3 car piggy banks and gladly handed over the PSL fees, as Carolina raised somewhere around $150 million. This became the template for any franchise looking to squeeze a few more dollars out of its most allegiant customers for a new stadium (or renovations for an old one). The Cincinnati Bengals sold PSLs for Paul Brown Stadium, becoming the first nonexpansion or nonrelocated team to do so. Fresno State University charged as much as $5,000 for PSLs in its Save Mart Center basketball arena. And then there was Ravenna High School in Ohio, which charged fans up to $1,500 for two seats at a new football stadium. Fans who purchased PSLs even got their names engraved on their seats.

So what's the big deal with PSLs? One word, eight letters: courtesy. (Full disclosure: It was 10 letters before I spell-checked it.) Before the scourge of PSLs, season-ticket holders had gentlemen's agreements with their teams regarding the very issues that the licenses legislate. You didn't need to spend $5,000 to ensure you got your seat the following season—you just got it. You didn't need to pony up a couple grand for the right to give your kid the season tickets—you just transferred them.

But what's building good will with your fans worth, compared with a one-time fee for the "privilege" to purchase a ticket to the game?

The Death of Organ Music
Turn That %#$% Down!

MADONNA ONCE sang that "music makes the people come together." While typing that line just made my fingers feel dirty for some reason, Maddie does have a point: six simple tones from an organ can provoke a Pavlovian burst of motivation from 18,000 fans.

Over time, organists added a few popular standards to their repertoire, such as "Happy Birthday to You" and "If You're Happy and You Know It" and several other songs that are supposed to bring a smile to your face even if your team's down by 50 in the fourth quarter. Then came the arena DJ, and soon sports organ music went the way of day baseball and fans attending games in their Sunday best.

There were some benefits: can anyone envision what live sporting events were like before "We Will Rock You" and "Rock and Roll Part II?" But there were some insidious side effects: can anyone envision what live sporting events were like before "YMCA" and "Who Let the Dogs Out?"

The real problem isn't with the fan-participation songs; it's with the music after every timeout or, lately, stoppage of play. That's the sort of thing that hampers the natural reactions and responses from crowds during a game. How hard is it to get a chant going with Metallica's "Enter Sandman" blaring from the arena sound system? Hell, how hard is it to talk to the guy next to you about the last play under the same conditions?

In the last decade, arenas have started literally adding a soundtrack to NBA games, blasting the backbeats from hip-hop and rock songs as offensive players bring the ball up the court. Does this do anything to enhance the fan experience? When Michael Jordan was defying gravity in the early 1990s, did any of us sit there and think, "Yeah, that foul-line dunk was OK and all . . . but what it really needed was the backbeat from Digital Underground's 'The Humpty Dance.'"

A more serious issue is at play here. Organ music was by and large homogenous populist fluff. Modern-day arena music is clearly tailored for the perceived audience for the sport: hip-hop for NBA games, alternative and classic rock at NHL games. In a time in which professional sports are doing all they can to break down societal barriers in order to reach new fans, doesn't the inherent racism of these musical selections fly in the face of that thinking? In other words, perhaps some hockey fans enjoy rap music . . . and, furthermore, aren't (gasp!) white!

If you're like me, you follow sports with an almost religious fervor. So shouldn't our churches echo with organ music?

Nobody Night

Baseball in Front of Empty Seats—
No, the Marlins Aren't Playing

YOU COULD conduct a focus group in a crack house at three o'clock in the morning and still not get ideas crazier than those put forth by minor-league baseball marketing departments.

Some promotions mimic current events, such as Triple-A Portland's Arthur Andersen Night in 2002, which celebrated the scandalous accounting firm by handing out receipts for $10 to every fan who purchased a $5 ticket. Some promotions are downright political, such as in 2002 when the St. Paul Saints gave away seat cushions that had MLB Players Association boss Donald Fehr on one side and commissioner Bud Selig on the other. Others are just nonsensical, like the Altoona Curve's Awful Night in 2003, which attempted to create the worst atmosphere for a baseball game ever by pumping in William Shatner music and reversing batting averages into "failed averages"— making a .350 hitter a .650 failure.

Then there are the promotions that try to leave a mark on the history books. Such was Nobody Night, a 2002 Charleston, South Carolina, Riverdogs promotion cooked up by radio play-by-play man Jim Lucas after he attended a seminar on promotion by team co-owner Mike Veeck (the man who nearly once held a Vasectomy Night at the stadium until it was canceled hours after it was announced). Lucas claimed that the record for lowest attendance at a professional baseball game was 12 fans, set at a rain-soaked game in 1881. So he suggested that the Riverdogs attempt to break the mark by playing an official game in front of an empty stadium.

On July 8, 2002, the Single-A Charleston played host to the Columbus RedStixx. Media, scouts, and employees were allowed to enter the stadium, but the gates were locked for the fans. They were instead ushered over to a huge party outside the ballpark with discounted food and beer. After five innings—and an official game—the fans were allowed into the stadium, with the attendance recorded as zero.

Great idea, right? Not so fast—according to ESPN, which contacted a representative with the research department of the National Baseball Hall of Fame, attendance is tabulated by tickets sold; thus Nobody Night was actually A Few Hundred Night. Oops.

Undeterred, the Riverdogs tried to set a different record the following season: the quietest game ever played. Silent Night was held on July 14, 2003, and for five innings featured fans holding up signs that said "Yeah!" "Boo!" and "Hey, Beer Man!" Oh, and for those who felt as though they couldn't keep their yaps shut—there was duct tape handy as well.

DOUBLE DRIBBLES AND AIR BALLS

PART 6

The Draft Lottery

Last-Place Teams Screwed by Ping-Pong Balls

IN 1992, the Minnesota Timberwolves were clearly the NBA's worst team. The third-year franchise won just 15 games for an embarrassing .183 winning percentage (the lowest of all-time was .110 by Philadelphia in 1972–1973).

Help appeared to be on the way, however, in the form of a hulking post player named Shaquille O'Neal, the nation's top collegiate prospect out of Louisiana State University. He was as close to a sure-thing draft pick as the league had seen since Patrick Ewing came out of Georgetown in 1985.

That was the year of the first NBA Draft Lottery, created by the league's Board of Governors at a 1984 meeting. In 1985, the Knicks (24–58) won the first lottery and leapfrogged over Indiana (22–60) and Golden State (22–60) for the top pick. It was a conspiracy theorist's wet dream: that the league had rigged the lottery to reinvigorate its lowly New York franchise with the can't-miss Ewing. This theory has evolved into the sports version of the Roswell crash, with the NBA claiming the 1985 lottery was just a weather balloon or swamp gas.

Seven years later, the T-Wolves appeared primed to draft the next great NBA center in Shaq . . . until the lottery changed their fortunes. The Orlando Magic (21–61) were given the first pick, selecting O'Neal; the Charlotte Hornets (31–51) also picked ahead of 15-win Minnesota, taking future all-star

Alonzo Mourning of Georgetown. The Timberwolves settled for Christian Laettner of Duke at No. 3.

But the real outrage of the lottery system that year was the fact that the Houston Rockets (42–40) actually had a 1-in-66 chance to pass all three of those doormats and draft the best amateur player in the nation—despite missing the playoffs by only a single game.

Is this really fair?

The NBA, WNBA, and NHL all employ lottery systems for their entry drafts as a safeguard against nonplayoff teams intentionally losing games to finish last and gain the top pick. It may be no coincidence that the NHL's first lottery was in 1995, four years after the Quebec Nordiques stumbled to the finish and just happened to earn the right to draft prodigy Eric Lindros at No. 1. And it may have been completely random that the NBA's lottery began the year after Houston got Akeem Olajuwon at No. 1, Chicago took Michael Jordan at No. 3, and Portland took Sam Bowie . . . oh, never mind about that one.

Hockey's lottery system at least makes an infinitesimal amount of sense. Nonplayoff teams that win the lottery can only advance four positions, ensuring that the worst team in the league drafts no worse than second overall. The NBA's lottery system is asinine. How does it help the league if the 17th best team has the opportunity to pick ahead of the 30th best team, even if there is just a 0.5 percent chance of that happening? The league is so obsessed with protecting against forced futility that it fails to ensure help for its truly futile teams.

Consider this: the NBA "refined" its draft lottery system in 1994, increasing the chances for teams with lower records to gain the No. 1 pick. In the next eight drafts, the team with the worst record in the league failed to secure the top pick overall every time. Pathetic . . .

The College Three-Point Shot
Killing the Transition Game since 1986

IT'S A COLLEGE basketball scenario that'll make your brain throb more than an all-nighter at Tappa Kegga. The opposing team misses a shot, and your team grabs the rebound and quickly moves into its transition offense. It's a three-on-two the other way! The crowd is buzzing! And then . . . some douchebag sophomore guard pulls up and clangs an ill-advised three-pointer off the iron and into the other team's hands.

Crowd? Subdued. Momentum? Dead.

"Ill-advised three-pointer" may be the ultimate oxymoron in men's college basketball. How a group of athletes who aren't responsible enough to be legally trusted to purchase a bottle of Goldschlager are expected to resist the siren's song of the three-point shot is beyond me. The poorly timed trifecta is as entrenched a tradition in college basketball as cheerleaders, student sections, and madness—be it midnight, March, or Bobby Knight's.

For the 1986–1987 season, the NCAA instituted the three-point shot (19 feet, 9 inches away from the basket) as a reaction to increasingly brutal play in the paint. The "three" would extend offenses and in turn bring defenders out from inside the lane to guard them. *Sports Illustrated* writer Alexander Wolff pinpointed the players who immediately benefited from the three-point shot: "Skinny little pencil-necked jump shooters who would be reduced to playing intramural Dungeons & Dragons if it weren't for the infernal work of their faculty advisor, Springfield College professor Edward Steitz, and his NCAA Rules Committee."

So the nerds got revenge on their broad-shouldered, post-playing pals by hoisting up as many long bombs as they could. By 2002, college players took one out of every three shots from behind the arc but made just 34.5 percent of them. Fifteen years earlier, that percentage was 38.4, as players took a three once out of every 6.4 field goal attempts.

Who could blame them? At 19-9, the college three was considered a layup when compared with the international (20-6) or NBA (23-9) three-point lines. The three replaced the dunk as the most electrifying shot in college hoops. More important, it allowed teams with limited athletic ability (read: Ivy League teams) to contend against more talented rivals. No schoolyard one-on-one breakdown moves needed; just square up, shoot, and hope to God one of the other skinny white kids grabs the board when you miss.

But whatever benefits the three-point shot offers, the fact remains that it is a hypocritical betrayal of the most basic tenets of the college game: fundamentals.

Defensively, the three-pointer takes away the thrill of individual battles, both in the paint and to the hoop. How do players practice defending a three-pointer? "Jump and pray" drills? Offensively, a player earns 50 percent more points from hitting a circus shot than for breaking down the defense for a dunk. It is like giving quarterbacks 30 yards for every 20-yard pass; the 10-yard slant pattern would be a distant memory.

For coaches, the college three is as destructive as it is distracting. Is there anything more frustrating for a fan than seeing the last 20 seconds of a near blowout stretched to absurdity by some coach who thinks he can play "three-foul-three-foul-three-foul" to erase a hole his team was inept enough to dig for itself in the first place?

There's been some talk of extending the college three-point line to the international distance or beyond. But that's like putting a Band-Aid on a decapitation victim. Perhaps the only thing that the NCAA can do is make a half-court shot worth more than any other distance; that way, "skinny little pencil-necked jump shooters" will start taking ill-advised fours instead of threes.

Alternating Possession

Who Really Wants the Excitement of a Jump Ball?

BASKETBALL IS a pleasant, simple game. Bounce the ball. Pass the ball. Throw the ball into the hoop. No wonder why all they needed back in the day was an empty peach basket and good weather.

Every controversial situation in basketball is resolved in an uncomplicated manner. If the ball goes out of bounds, you throw it back in. If you are about to score and some guy hacks your arm, you get a second chance to earn those points at a special line in front of the hoop with no one guarding you. If two players both think they have possession, the ball is tossed up in the air between them and they both jump up to settle the debate.

In 1982, the NCAA decided to needlessly confound that last predicament.

Alternating possession replaced the jump ball that year. A possession arrow, placed on the scorer's table, indicates which team receives the ball for a throw-in after every jump ball or held-ball situation. The team that lost the opening tip to begin the game receives the first possession arrow. For example, if a ball thrown in by Team A on an alternating possession call is held jointly by a player from Team A and one from Team B, then the alternating possession arrow is reversed and the ball is awarded to Team B at a designated spot

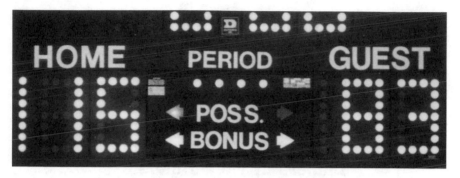

The dreaded possession arrow. (Courtesy of the Connection Newspapers archives)

on the floor. That's a hell of a lot easier than having two guys jump in the air, isn't it?

Pro-alternation advocates say that the referee simply can't be trusted to throw the ball up in a fair way, which would be a hell of an argument if these rogue officials weren't already entrusted to make every other decision in the damn game. The only half-sane argument ever made in defense of alternating possession is that jump balls frequently feature a post player of considerable height facing off against an undersized guard. Well, let me throw out two names: John "Hot Plate" Williams versus Spud Webb.

Case closed. Alternating possession sucks.

High School Players in the NBA

Should Teams Have to Include Diapers in Their Budgets?

IF I HAD a bar bet to prove that prep stars in the NBA is one of the truly worst ideas in sports history, I might not take it. The guy sitting next to me nursing his scotch could simply mumble, "Kobe Bryant, Kevin Garnett, Tracy McGrady, LeBron James," and I'd be knocked off my stool onto my arse. But this isn't a bar bet; it's a book—which means that we can go beyond the superficial eight-word answer and get to the heart of the matter, which is how much Jonathan Bender sucks.

Bender was a hell of player . . . back when his primary scoring concern was his prom date. He averaged 23.1 points per game and 15 rebounds as a high school senior in Picayune, Mississippi. He broke Michael Jordan's scoring record in the 1999 McDonald's High School All-America Game, scoring 31 to MJ's 30. Bender signed a letter of intent to join Mississippi State's men's basketball program but instead opted to enter the 1999 NBA draft. And why not: better pay, better hotels, and hot hoops groupies interested in finding out more about both.

But Bender was a high school player. A project. Even if he were a Cadillac, he would have been sitting on cinder blocks with no engine and both doors missing. That didn't stop the Toronto Raptors from taking him fifth overall, ahead of Richard Hamilton (7), Andre Miller (8), and Ron Artest (16). It also didn't stop the Indiana Pacers from trading starting post player Antonio Davis for Bender after the draft.

The results are in, and the Pacers are idiots. In six seasons (through 2004–2005), Bender averaged 5.6 points and a pathetic 2.2 rebounds per game. The only reason that he couldn't be called a bust was the fact that Kwame Brown (Glynn Academy High School, class of 2001) still had a job in the league.

Imagine how life would have been different for Bender had he played even three years in the NCAA? Then again, imagine how life would have been different for the NCAA if players like Bender, Kobe, McGrady, LeBron, Garnett, Amare Stoudemire, Jermaine O'Neal, Darius Miles, Tyson Chandler, Eddy Curry, and the eight high school players who were drafted in the top 20 of the 2004 draft had chosen college over the pros? Even if they only played two seasons—the days of four-year scholars such as Tim Duncan may never return—their impact on individual programs could have changed the face of the NCAA. Perhaps collegiate men's basketball would be more than three or four meaningful regular season games and a giant excuse for an office pool in March . . .

It's not just college basketball that's been devastated by the influx of high school players in the NBA. Ever hear of DeAngelo Collins, Lenny Cooke, Giedrius Rinkevicius, Tony Key, Ellis Richardson, or Taj McDavid? All of them were high school stars who declared for the NBA draft. None of them were drafted. Dick Vitale refers to them as "basketball vagabonds." I'm pretty sure one of them pumped my gas the other day.

The NBA finally got it right when it negotiated a new collective bargaining agreement with the players in 2005, demanding that rookies wait one year after their high school class had graduated to be eligible for the draft (international players had to be 19 years or older). It's a decision that will help the pro game as well as several lower levels of basketball, like the college ranks and the National Basketball Development League.

The Field of 65

Suddenly, the NIT Champ Is the 66th Best Team in America

THE NATIONAL Collegiate Athletic Association. The NCAA. Founded in 1906 as the Intercollegiate Athletic Association of the United States, it's a voluntary cooperative of about 1,200 colleges and universities, athletic conferences, and sports organizations. Unofficial motto? "Dedicated to finding new and inventive ways to screw the little guy."

The NCAA's most egregious offenses against the have-nots are often at the expense of the "mid-major" conferences—for example, when it gives Pop Warner teams more respect in the Bowl Championship Series than it does a team from the Mountain West Conference. Even when the NCAA appears to hear the mid-majors' calls for fairness, it's like those times when you ask someone to give you a hand and the dumb ass starts clapping.

In 1975, the NCAA men's basketball championship tournament grew to a field of 32. This enabled the selection committee to choose a second team from any conference as an "at large" bid. The expansion proved so successful that the tournament field ballooned to 48 by 1980 and then to 64 in 1985. For years, mid-major tournament champions—from regions like the Mid-Eastern Athletic Conference and the Patriot League—simply accepted their automatic bid to the Big Dance and the subsequent first-round ass kicking from a top seed. In 2001, the NCAA smelled fresh money to be made, so it decided to expand the field again to 65 and have the two lowest seeds—ranked by the ratings percentage index—compete in a "play-in game" on the Tuesday after selection Sunday.

For the NCAA, the idea had little downside. It added an extra televised tournament game. It added another at-large bid for a major conference to grab. Best of all, it would force two mid-major champs into the Thunderdome of March Madness: two weak sisters enter; only one of them leaves.

How does this screw the little guy, you ask? Look at the 2004 tournament play-in game. Florida A&M battled back from a 1–10 start to win the Mid-Eastern Athletic Conference tournament. Lehigh won the Patriot League and earned its first tournament berth in 16 years. Yet they had to win another game to earn a slot on the printable bracket. It's like finishing four years of college and then being required to take an extra physics class on statistical mechanics and thermodynamics before you can get your diploma. (Of course, over 50 percent of college ballers think a diploma is something that you use to check your motor oil.) The play-in games themselves have been virtually ignored. The 2004 game only drew around 7,800 fans to a 13,266-seat arena. The 2005 game saw a crowd of 8,254 in the University of Dayton's 13,455-seat arena—and that was with a team from Michigan in the game. In its first four years, the team winning this borderline exhibition has gone on to lose by an average of 24 points in the first round of the tournament.

As with many unsound ideas in sports, this one could work if reimagined. Instead of having two doormats play for the right to get their asses handed to them by Duke in the 1-versus-16 game, why not have the play-in game pit the two lowest-seeded at-large teams from conferences like the ACC and the Big East against each other, with a No. 10 seed on the line? It'd be a more compelling TV game, and the winner might actually have a fighting chance in the next round.

But it's the NCAA, so the odds are better that we'll have a field of 80 before the play-in game is remedied.

The American Basketball League

Turns Out That Two Women's Leagues Were One Too Many

OPERATING FROM 1978 until it folded in 1981, the Women's Basketball League was the first female pro hoops league in America, with teams such as the Milwaukee Does and the Minnesota Fillies. (This was clearly before the advent of political correctness and PETA protests.)

The following 15 years were a boom time for women's basketball and female sports in general. Title IX gained prominence and influence, the catalyst for hundreds of thousands of young women participating in high school and collegiate sports. NCAA women's basketball grew in popularity and television exposure. The U.S. Women's Basketball National Team went on a 14-month tour of the country, leading up to its gold medal–winning performance at the 1996 Summer Olympics in Atlanta.

The time was right for another professional women's basketball league to take its shot. The American Basketball League began play in 1996 with eight teams: some in NBA cities such as Seattle and Atlanta and others in places such as Richmond and Columbus.

One teensy little problem: There was this giant red, white, and blue elephant sitting in the corner of the room named the WNBA, set to debut in summer 1997. The NBA-backed league had franchises in New York and Los Angeles, national television exposure, bigger arenas, and some guy named David Stern leading its marketing assault. I hear he did some work with Michael Jordan back in the day.

The groundwork for the ABL was being laid in 1995, back when the WNBA's arrival may not have seemed like impending doom. But as soon as the NBA decided to create a league of its own, ABL management should have met for drinks, begrudgingly spoke of what could have been, and then began preparing their resumes for delivery to Mr. Stern's office the following morning.

The ABL didn't have a prayer against its rival league, even with a year's head start. The WNBA had television deals with NBC, ABC, ESPN, and Lifetime, which actually found time between made-for-TV movies about philandering husbands to show a basketball game. The ABL had deals with SportsChannel (ask the NHL how that went), FOX Sports Net, and, in its last season, CBS for two championship-round playoff games.

The WNBA had a marketing budget of $15 million; the ABL's was about $2.6 million. That meant huge exposure for WNBA teams and stars and some lopsided attendance figures between the two leagues. By 1998, the WNBA averaged 10,729 fans to the ABL's 4,333. Even the Washington Mystics, 3–27 in 1998, drew over 15,000 fans per game.

A major factor behind the WNBA's success at the gate was timing—as a summer league, it had easy television clearance and scores of young fans with nothing else better to do during vacation. The ABL played during the winter in a sports market flooded with football, hockey, playoff baseball, and college and pro basketball. It was like trying to hold an Easter-egg hunt on Christmas morning.

The ABL was a failure, folding midseason in December 1998 and filing for Chapter 11 bankruptcy protection. But it was a noble failure, as many postmortem press accounts acknowledged. The overall play in the league was better than that of the WNBA. The players were fundamentally sound and gritty, determined to make the league work. There was something heart-warming about the grassroots, pioneer spirit of the league and its fans.

But there's a tremendous difference between a leap of faith and a suicide jump. With two women's basketball leagues vying for the same limited fan base—and with one of the two backed by the NBA—the ABL was doomed from the start.

Five-Game Playoffs in the NBA

Hey Gang . . . Let's Punish Success, Shall We?

NBA REGULAR season games have about as much relevance as the scripted scenes in a pornographic film: we all know why they exist, but we're more than willing to skip 'em to get to the good stuff (and by good stuff, I mean the intercourse . . . in the porno, not in the NBA).

The five-game playoff series did what, at times, seemed impossible to do: make the NBA regular season even more pointless than it already was. Take 1994's epic battle between the Seattle Supersonics and the Denver Nuggets. Seattle didn't just have the best record in the Western Conference; the Sonics were the best team in the entire NBA at 63–19. The team boasted stars such as Shawn Kemp (before his fat-Elvis phase), Gary Payton (before his flame-out with the Lakers), and Detlef Schrempf (before one out of every three players in the NBA had a name like Detlef Schrempf).

Seattle took the first two games at home from No. 8–seeded Denver. But then the Nuggets won twice to tie the series at 2–2 and send it back to the cradle of Starbucks for Game 5. Amazingly, Denver won that game 98–94 in overtime, completing the first opening-round series victory for a No. 8 seed since the NBA adopted the five-game playoff format in 1984.

It was one time too many. Think about it: had it been the second round or the conference championship or the NBA Finals, Seattle would have had two more chances to save its successful season. But a three-game losing streak in Round 1 eliminated what was, by far, the best team in the NBA regular season.

The league finally wised up in 2003, establishing a seven-game series in the opening round. Critics slammed the change in format as the "Laker Rule," as the decision appeared to favor veteran teams such as Los Angeles that were built for longer series rather than five-game sprints.

But why shouldn't it? Isn't it in the best interest of the NBA and its fans to have the biggest stars and the most intriguing teams playing deep into the postseason? To actually give winning teams, you know, an advantage?

What about the little guy, you say?

You know what? Screw the little guy. The haves get a seven-game first-round series; the have-nots get the Draft Lottery. And the fans, more often than not, get their money shot . . . er, money's worth.

Allowing the Clippers to Draft Anyone
Los Angeles Has Some Huge Busts

BEVERLY HILLS real estate mogul Donald Sterling purchased the San Diego Clippers in 1981. As of the 2004–2005 season, the franchise has managed only one season above .500.

Yes, the words *Clippers* and *suck* have enjoyed a long and happy consanguinity, first in San Diego and then, beginning in 1984, as the "other team" in Los Angeles. As if Sterling wasn't inept enough, he hired Elgin Baylor in 1986 to be the Clippers' vice president of basketball operations, aka the first mate of the *Titanic*, forever diminishing his status as a Hall of Famer.

Through a series of high draft picks, the NBA keeps trying to give the Clippers a franchise player; through a series of bad decisions, the Clippers keep refusing to select one, like a syphilis patient rejecting penicillin. Even the marginally talented players they drafted either left as soon as they were free agents or were packaged in disastrous trades. Some lowlights in Clippers' draft history follow:

1982

Drafted: Terry Cummings, DePaul, at No. 2 overall.
Ignored: Dominique Wilkins (Utah, No. 3).
Even worse: After averaging over 20 points per game in two seasons, Cummings was traded with Ricky Pierce and Craig Hodges for Marques Johnson, Harvey Catchings, Junior Bridgeman, and cash. All three were out of the league by 1989; Pierce played until 1998, Cummings until 2000.

1984

Drafted: Lancaster Gordon, Louisville, at No. 8 overall.
Ignored: Otis Thorpe (Kansas City, No. 9), Kevin Willis (Atlanta, No. 11), and John Stockton (Utah, No. 16).
Even worse: Gordon was waived after four seasons after averaging 5.4 points per game as a pro. He later told the *Louisville Courier-Journal*, "I don't feel like the Clippers ever wanted or needed my set of skills."

1985

Drafted: Benoit Benjamin, Creighton, at No. 3 overall.
Ignored: Chris Mullin (Golden State, No. 7), Detlef Schrempf (Dallas, No. 8), Charles Oakley (Cleveland, No. 9), Karl Malone (Utah, No. 13), Joe Dumars (Detroit, No. 18), A. C. Green (Los Angeles Lakers, No. 23), and Terry Porter (Portland, No. 24).
Even worse: Can it get any worse?

1987

Drafted: Reggie Williams, Georgetown, at No. 4 overall.
Ignored: Scottie Pippen (Seattle, No. 5), Kevin Johnson (Cleveland, No. 7), Reggie Miller (Indiana, No. 11), and Mark Jackson (New York, No. 18).
Even worse: Williams played two unremarkable seasons with the Clip until getting shipped with Danny Ferry to Cleveland. Speaking of whom . . .

1989

Drafted: Danny Ferry, Duke, at No. 2 overall.
Ignored: Sean Elliott (San Antonio, No. 3), Glen Rice (Miami, No. 4), Tim Hardaway (Golden State, No. 14), Shawn Kemp (Seattle, No. 17), and Vlade Divac (Lakers, No. 26).
Even worse: Ferry refused to sign with the abhorrent Clippers, opting to play a season for Il Messaggero Roma in Italy. Los Angeles finally got the messaggero and traded Ferry and Williams to the Cavaliers for Ron Harper and a package.

1995

Drafted: Antonio McDyess, Alabama, at No. 2 overall.
Ignored: Jerry Stackhouse (Philadelphia, No. 3), Rasheed Wallace (Washington, No. 4), Kevin Garnett (Minnesota, No. 5), and Damon Stoudamire (Toronto, No. 7).
Even worse: For the second time in six years, the Clippers waste the second overall pick in the draft on a player that never suited up for them. McDyess was traded to Denver for Rodney Rogers and Brent Barry.

1998

Drafted: Michael Olowokandi, Pacific, at No. 1 overall.
Ignored: Antawn Jamison (Toronto, No. 4), Vince Carter (Golden State, No. 5), Dirk Nowitzki (Milwaukee, No. 9), and Paul Pierce (Boston, No. 10).
Even worse: The "Kandi Man" made a list of the biggest draft busts of all time in 2003, the same year he signed a three-year, $16 million free-agent contract with Minnesota.

You can't fault them for Danny Manning at No. 1 overall in 1988. But you sure as hell can fault them for Terry Dehere (No. 13, 1993) over Sam Cassell; Lamond Murray (No. 7, 1994) over Eddie Jones and Jalen Rose; and Lorenzen Wright (No. 7, 1996) over Kerry Kittles, Steve Nash, Jermaine O'Neal, Derek Fisher, and some guy named Kobe. Maybe one year while they're drafting, the Clippers will do their fans a favor and simply let the clock run out . . .

LIARS!

PART 7

Rosie Ruiz "Wins" the Marathon

Cheaters Never Prosper . . . Unless They Get Caught

WHEN IT comes to cheating, there are varying degrees of severity. Think about your high school years. Copying the odd answers out of the back of your algebra book was less severe than glancing over at your classmate's answer sheet during a quiz, which itself wasn't as bad as stealing a copy of that quiz the day before you had to take it.

My most severe case of cheating (that I'm willing to admit) was in physics class. I didn't know dick about physics, other than how fast you needed to swing a bat to hit a curve ball. So I may have let the ol' peepers gaze over a friend's shoulder once or twice during an exam. My teacher—who, like many male educators in his chosen course of study, had a face that resembled a South African burrowing bullfrog—suspected that my remarkable turnaround on said exam was in fact not a product of my studious nature but rather one of my wandering eyes. So he called me up to his desk and asked me if my answers were my own; I, of course, claimed they were. Then he decided to get cute, and he started to ask me questions off the exam, figuring I'd just stand there catching flies. And I would have, save for one glorious flaw in Mr. Ribbit's plan: the answer key, which he accidentally left in plain view in front of me on his desk. So with each question, I'd drop my head, "searching" for an answer and then miraculously coming up with the right one. After three questions, I had him convinced that I was Blaise Pascal.

It was a quality ruse. Yet compared with what Rosie Ruiz pulled off in the 1980 Boston Marathon, I was a paragon of virtue. The 26-year-old Ruiz entered the race having taken 11th overall in the New York Marathon. On April 21, 1980, she finished the Boston Marathon in 2 hours, 31 minutes, and 56 seconds—the third-fastest time in history for a female runner.

But there was something fishier than a vat of New England clam chowder about Ruiz's victory. Like the fact that she wasn't exactly "tired" or "sweaty" after having run a marathon. Or her answer when men's marathon winner Bill Rodgers asked her what her splits were: "What are splits?" Or the fact that neither the other runners nor the checkpoint officials nor the race marshals could recall seeing her for most of the 26.2-mile course. Or the fact that photographers and videographers and surveillance cameras all failed to capture her image as she ran the race. (Ruiz would claim that she had been confused for a male runner because of her short hair.)

In the days following the race, several eyewitnesses revealed that they had witnessed Ruiz suddenly enter the race's final half-mile. Others claimed that she had veered off course near the start of the race and "ran" most of the event by riding the subway. Similar charges were levied against Ruiz from eyewitnesses in New York about her marathon performance there. Based on the evidence—and ignoring Ruiz's continued defiance—race officials disqualified her and elevated Jackie Gareau of Canada into first place.

In the years following her controversial "victory" in Boston, Ruiz spent a week in a New York jail for stealing from the real estate company where she was employed; later, she was arrested on charges that she sold cocaine to undercover agents in Miami. Ruiz, now known as Rosie Vivas, remained in Florida . . . and remains adamant about having won the Boston Marathon fair and square. She claims that her "win" was a landmark moment for women in sports and that she has received evidence from supporters that verifies she ran and completed the race.

Right . . . just like I could give you the formula for tangential velocity off the top of my head.

Tom Lockhart Reports
Fake Games
League Promoter Turns into Fiction Writer

THOMAS F. LOCKHART is in the Hockey Hall of Fame because— among his other significant accomplishments—in 1936 he founded the Amateur Hockey Association of the United States, known today as USA Hockey. Thomas F. Lockhart is in this book because the *F* can, in one notorious case, easily stand for *fraud*.

In the early 20th century, Lockhart was a promoter at Madison Square Garden, home to three amateur hockey teams that played on weekend afternoons. In 1933, he successfully lobbied the Tri-State Hockey League to include his teams on its schedule, and the new Eastern Amateur Hockey League began operation that year.

In the league's first season, 48 home games were to be played at the Garden by the three New York teams. Slight problem: MSG only had 16 available dates on Sundays for the league, making it impossible for the EHL to finish its regular season. Never have Tom Lockhart book your wedding.

So Lockhart did what any other rational human being would do in his situation: he just made a bunch of stuff up. According to writer Chuck Miller in

Hockey Ink! magazine, Lockhart invented 21 games, reporting phony box scores and results to local newspapers. That's right: fiction in the *New York Times* 70 years before Jayson Blair. The promoter even tried to cover his bases by claiming the extra home games had been "played during practice hours at the Garden" and were not open to the public. Lockhart can't be accused of being too disingenuous, though; despite inventing nearly two dozen home games, his three Big Apple teams still ended up a combined 10–43–17 on the season.

The stunt may have helped the EHL "complete" its important inaugural season, but it remains one of the only black marks on an otherwise stellar career for a true pioneer in American hockey. Of course, Lockhart almost redeemed himself by having ice-skating grizzly bears as between-periods entertainment.

Almost . . .

Lying on Your Coaching Résumé

What Do You Mean by "Checking My References"?

GEORGE O'LEARY could be my football coach any day. He's successful, with a career winning percentage over .600 as a collegiate head coach before taking over at Central Florida in 2004. But more important, he can parse words and manipulate the English language in a way that would have made John Kerry blush.

O'Leary strikes me as the kind of coach who would call a loss a "nonvictory" or a fumble an "unfortunate malfunction of possession." What else could be expected from the man who dismissed audacious lying on his résumé with such colloquial brush-offs as "inaccuracies" and "misstatements"?

O'Leary left a winning program at Georgia Tech in 2001 to become the new head coach at the University of Notre Dame. His new school used the same biographical information that O'Leary had been using since his days as an assistant coach at Syracuse University, back in 1980. But five days after he was hired, O'Leary was forced to resign when the *Union Leader* (Manchester, New Hampshire) reported that he had fabricated a football career at the University of New Hampshire in his bio. Instead of earning three letters during his time at the school, O'Leary actually never played a single game. An honest mistake . . . for a moron. But for O'Leary, a whopper of a fib. O'Leary also was "inaccurate" when he claimed that he earned a master's degree from New York University in 1972. Because he didn't.

In the grand scheme of things, O'Lie . . . er . . . O'Leary's "misstatements" weren't so bad. Heck, his "inaccuracies" don't even sink to the pathetic lows of former Toronto Blue Jays manager Tim Johnson.

Johnson repeatedly told players in Toronto, and before that in Boston, tales about the hell that was war in Vietnam, where he allegedly served as a U.S. Marine. He was indeed a member of the U.S. Marines but in the reserves . . . and he never exactly made it over to 'Nam. He did do a hell of a job training American soldiers who were headed to Vietnam about the intricacies of mortar technology—that is, when he wasn't shagging flies on the diamond.

"Friends of mine were going to Vietnam when I was going to spring training," he said in a December 1998 press conference, after his G. I. Joke routine was exposed. "While they were off fighting and getting killed, I was playing baseball." That didn't stop Johnson from pretending that he was in the trenches with them. For example, he decided to pump up Blue Jays pitcher Pat Hentgen before a game at Fenway Park by concocting a heartwarming story about killing two children in Vietnam because they were in the line of fire.

Johnson, who also falsely claimed on his official bio to have been a two-time all-American basketball player, was fired by the Blue Jays during spring training in 1999. In 2003, he finally served "in country" . . . in a country called Mexico to be exact, managing something called Yaquis de Obregon in the Mexican Pacific League.

Letting Pete Rose into Cooperstown
What Are the Odds of That?

IT'S GOING to happen, people. Maybe not in my lifetime, perhaps not in yours. Or, depending on how the stiff wind of sentimental revisionism is blowing, Pete Rose might be enshrined in the National Baseball Hall of Fame by the time you finish reading this sentence.

There's very little a baseball player could do that would warrant the kind of blackballing that Rose received in 1989, after he agreed to leave baseball for life. He agreed so that he didn't have to admit that he bet on games as a manager for the Cincinnati Reds (despite overwhelming evidence that he had done so). Think about it: We've embraced potheads and cokeheads. We've cheered players who have been caught artificially altering their bats and their bodies. Taken at face value, the question becomes, was Pete Rose's betting on baseball after his playing days were over really that much more nefarious than Barry Bonds's admission—via leaked grand-jury testimony—that he used steroids (unknowingly, of course, . . . tee-hee) during his string of record-breaking home-run seasons?

Well, yes, actually it is.

Those sluggers on the juice cheated, no question about that. But at no point did baseball fans drop their hard-earned money for a ticket to the game and have to wonder if the outcome of that game had been predetermined by the performance-enhanced players on either roster. They still had to hit the ball. They still had eight other players in the lineup with them. But when a baseball manager is betting on or against his own team, the integrity of the game is threatened in a way a player cannot threaten it. The manager determines who those players are and when they play. He can manipulate a lineup or a pitching rotation to ensure an outcome that will win him a wager, even at the expense of his own team. And that's far more damaging to the virtue of baseball than a player lathering himself in steroid cream.

In Rose's case, a number of fans, journalists, and ex-players were actually willing to forgive his betting ways over time. Then he decided to take commissioner Bud Selig's bait and admit in a 2004 book that he bet on baseball as manager of the Reds. It was an act of contrition meant to grease the wheels for his reinstatement; instead, he copped to compulsively lying for 15 years and continued to rationalize the motivations behind his sins. Rose's public support eroded faster than his hairline.

The only case that can still be made for Rose's enshrinement in Cooperstown is based on his contributions as a player—that 4,256 hits and a career .303 batting average over 24 seasons trump his transgressions as a manager.

That case is, of course, the kind of touchy-feely nostalgic baseball bullshit that makes me want to kick people like Bob Costas in the nuts. Back in the grown-up world, there are fairly cut-and-dry rules that govern such matters as managers who bet on their own teams . . . such as Rule 21 (d) in Major League Baseball, which states that "any player, umpire, or club or league official or employee, who shall bet any sum whatsoever upon any baseball game in connection with which the bettor has a duty to perform shall be declared permanently ineligible." And then there's that pesky Rule 3 (e) in the Rules for Election to the National Baseball Hall of Fame by Members of the Baseball Writers' Association of America, which states, "Any player on Baseball's ineligible list shall not be an eligible candidate."

No one on MLB's ineligible list has ever been reinstated. That includes New York Giants outfielder Benny Kauff, who was banned in 1921 after being indicted on charges of auto theft, a crime for which he was later acquitted.

Are we really going to let the guy who bet on the team he was managing into the Hall before the guy who didn't steal a car?

SOCCER SUCKAGE

PART 8

Mutiny in the Name of Victory
When Scoring into Your Own Net Is Actually Encouraged

YOU NEED a protractor and a Pentagon supercomputer to figure out championship soccer tournaments. All of those groups, pools, points, differentials . . . players already can't use their damn hands; why complicate life even more?

Some soccer tournaments feel as though their labyrinthine structure simply isn't confusing enough, so they create a few confounded rules and regulations to accompany it. For example, tournaments frequently use goals scored and surrendered as a tiebreaker, so scoring is encouraged and, since most soccer matches are the athletic equivalent of NyQuil, this is a good thing—but not if the rules force players to begin scoring *against* their own team.

The Shell Caribbean Cup, now called the Caribbean Nations Cup, was a qualifying tournament for the Confederation of North, Central American, and Caribbean Football Gold Cup. In 1994, a preliminary match between Barbados and Grenada was to determine which team would advance to the final grouping of the Caribbean tournament. The teams were in a dead heat in the standings—Barbados had to win the match by a minimum of two goals to place above Grenada and earn a trip to the finals. If it didn't, Grenada would win the group and the berth.

Grenada scored in the second half to cut Barbados's lead to 2–1 with less than seven minutes left in the match. I forgot to tell you an important note about the tournament's idiotic format: any team that won in sudden-death overtime was automatically credited with a two-goal victory. Knowing this, and leading by just one goal, Barbados scored on its own net to tie the game with about three minutes left in regulation.

Ah, but the futbol tomfoolery didn't end there! Grenada attempted to break the tie it never created by trying to score into *its* own goal, to avoid overtime and to secure the finals' berth via goal differential. But Barbados began defending Grenada's net as well as its own goal (talk about playing on both sides of the football), and regulation ended with the teams tied, 2–2. Barbados scored four minutes into overtime, winning the match "by two" and handing Grenada a one-way ticket to elimination.

MLS in the Sunshine State
Futbol Es No Muy Bueno en Florida

MAJOR LEAGUE Soccer placed two of its franchises in Florida: the Tampa Bay Mutiny (1996) and the Miami Fusion (1998). Both teams were financial and attendance disasters, and both were contracted in 2002. Why didn't they work? Soccer thrived in the state during the 1970s, back in the North American Soccer League days with teams such as the Tampa Bay Rowdies—which is amazing when you consider how frickin' hot Florida is in the summer.

Oy, the humidity! Any state in which you need to "squeeze out" your shirt before you place it in a hamper has an excess water-vapor problem. It's a common misconception that the best things about the Sunshine State are its theme parks and its beaches; anyone who's been there in July will tell you it's actually the twin miracles of central and automotive air conditioning.

The weather was a factor (heck, they built a domed stadium in Tampa before they even had a baseball team to play in it). But it wasn't the only factor. The Fusion was supposed to be a flagship franchise for the fledgling league, not only due to the team's wide-open style of play, but also because of a simple equation: soccer + gigantic Latino community = mucho popularity, chico.

San Jose and D.C. United are two Major League Soccer teams that have thrived. (Pam Brooks)

But the "If you build it, they will *venir*" simply didn't translate. Perhaps the high immigrant population had seen too much good soccer to settle for MLS ball. Whatever the case, Miami drew 9,345 fans on average for four years—worst in MLS despite winning a regular-season conference championship in 2001.

Tampa Bay averaged 11,072 fans per game over six years, which was good enough for 10th out of 12 teams in the league. The team never had an independent owner; MLS bankrolled and supported the team for six years. It was like having a child who dropped out of college and then sponged off his parents for six years; finally, they just had to kick his ass out of the house. Of course, the fact that the team sucked for most of its existence didn't help matters. The only thing bigger than Tampa Bay's disappointment was the mop on star forward Carlos Valderrama's head.

The climate, the unique obstacles the teams faced . . . perhaps both circumstances were trumped by the very nature of Floridian sports fans. They like basketball teams and hockey teams that win, but the losing ones might as well be playing in Cuba. I'm not sure whether they know that they *have* baseball, even when the Marlins win the World Series. But they love football, college or pro, and they really love auto racing (must have something to do with the speed limits on the interstates down there).

So, basically, Floridian fans like sports that involve violent full contact and massive tailgating opportunities. While soccer offers the latter, maybe a few more red cards would have filled the stands—100 percent humidity notwithstanding.

PUCKING IDIOTS

PART 9

In the Crease, on the Video
Instant Replay Robs the Sabres

THE FIRST time I met NHL commissioner Gary Bettman was in 2002 at the Hockey Hall of Fame induction weekend in Toronto. Bettman and the league's Board of Governors had, in the off-season, encouraged ferocious enforcement of obstruction and roughing penalties. That resulted in power-play-laden games that had little quality checking and a spasmodic offensive flow.

That evening at the hall, emboldened by a few free cocktails, I decided that I needed to have a chat with Mr. Bettman. About the draconian rule enforcement. About the way his league tried to use the "instigator" penalty to legislate fighting out of the sport in the 1990s, a time when violence was an unbeatable marketing tool in pro sports yet the NHL kept that arrow in its quiver. About the overexpansion, the underpromotion, and the rest of the blunders that had put the league on a path to irrelevance.

As Bettman walked away from the VIPs with whom he had been schmoozing, I made my move, approaching him on his right and extending my hand. "If it isn't Mr. Commissioner himself," I said jovially.

He ignored me and kept walking.

"Humph," I muttered.

"What?" asked the diminutive commish, his pace still brisk and his eyes locked forward.

"I just wanted to shake your hand," I said, still extending my right hand.

"How am I supposed to know you wanted to shake my hand?" said Bettman.

We shook, Bettman never making eye contact and never breaking stride. Time for some offense: "So, when are we going to bring fighting back to hockey?"

"We haven't changed the rules in 11 years," Bettman snapped back. How silly of me to consider adding a second referee (1998) to be a rule change.

"Haven't changed the . . . we're averaging 20 power plays a game this season. It's bad hockey!" I said. At this point, Bettman picked up speed, left me in his wake, and journeyed back to Middle-earth to join the rest of the Hobbits.

While Bettman's follies could have, on their own, encompassed the majority of the entries on this list, let's focus on one momentous blunder: instant video replay on "in the crease" violations. Beginning in the 1991–1992 season, referees were encouraged to be more vigilant against players who crashed the goalies' crease on offensive chances, particularly when their actions impaired the keeper and resulted in a goal. In 1997, Bettman's rules committee upped the ante by allowing referees to telephone an off-ice official and utilize slow-motion instant replays to determine if an offensive player had interfered with a goalie by illegally entering his crease. In the past, referees allowed goals if a player happened to dip his skate into the crease but did not affect the goalie in any way; now, it would warrant a goal being disallowed. The rule resulted in dozens of goals being refused for no other reason than a single skate in the crease. It also slowed the game to a crawl for several minutes as a little man in a skybox played with his editing equipment.

In 1999, the rule was the catalyst in one of the greatest miscarriages of justice in the history of hockey. In Game 6 of the Stanley Cup Finals between Dallas and Buffalo, Stars forward Brett Hull scored at 14 minutes, 51 seconds of the third overtime to win the cup for his team. But should it have counted? Hull took a shot; Sabres goalie Dominik Hasek made the save; the puck rebounded outside the crease; and Hull's skate came into the crease before his rebound shot beat Hasek. Buffalo players and coach Lindy Ruff were irate that Hull's skate was (clearly) illegally in the crease and that a video replay had never been requested by the referee. The NHL claimed that the play had been reviewed and the goal approved by off-ice officials, although the Buffalo PA announcer had never indicated to the crowd that the play was being reviewed—something customary for any examined goal.

As for Hull's skate being in the crease, Bettman crony Bryan Lewis, the NHL's director of officiating at the time, said that the goal was good because the officials "determined that Hull played the puck [and] had possession of the puck." Never mind the fact that a dozen similar cases had resulted in goals being disallowed during the regular season—none of them were being "reviewed" while the commissioner was polishing the Stanley Cup.

The NHL certainly seemed convinced that video replay had saved the day. So convinced, in fact, that it took only two days after Dallas won the cup for the Board of Governors to eliminate replay for "in the crease" violations. Welcome to Gary Bettman's NHL . . .

The Mighty Ducks of Anaheim
The NHL Goes Quackers

*T*HE BAD *News Bears* was a classic. Walter Matthau ruled as beer-swilling coach Morris Buttermaker. The kids spewed curses like my father used to when fixing the engine on his old Subaru hatchback. The guy behind *Fletch* and *Semi-Tough* directed it. And who doesn't love a movie in which a precocious Little League team is sponsored by Chico's Bail Bonds?

But if you had taken a poll of every Major League Baseball team in 1976, how many of them actually wanted to *be* the Bad News Bears? (Excuse the Montreal Expos, who at 55–107 almost were.) Seriously—the Bears couldn't win the big game, they had piss-colored uniforms, and their best player was a girl!

Fast forward to 1993. Disney Sports Enterprises, a division of the Walt Disney Company, decides to buy into the National Hockey League with an expansion team in Anaheim, California. The year before, Disney released *The Mighty Ducks*—a family-friendly, hockey-themed variation on *The Bad News Bears* formula—and it became a surprise hit.

Evidently, Michael Eisner saw no problem with professional hockey players wearing the same sweaters that a bunch of brats in an Emilio Estevez movie did. How proud 16-year-veteran and former Soviet star Anatoli Semenov must have been when he first laid eyes on that duck-shaped hockey mask logo with the mint green and yellow color scheme; one look and he was probably begging for a trip back to the gulag.

Disney expected the Mighty Ducks licensed merchandise to attract fans to the arena rather than have a winning franchise draw them in. Sales of T-shirts, jerseys, and hats were good; the team wasn't. The Mighty Ducks missed the playoffs in each of their first three seasons.

In 2003, the rest of the hockey world finally realized what a horrendous name Disney had infected the league with. Anaheim made the Stanley Cup Finals and was one win away from adding Mighty Ducks to names such as Canadiens, Red Wings, and Oilers on the greatest piece of championship hardware in sports.

Luckily, the New Jersey Devils dumped Anaheim in Game 7, and the NHL ducked a mighty embarrassment.

The Islanders Go Gorton's
Four Cups . . . Apparently Just for Tartar Sauce

THE MID-1990s weren't the greatest time to be a New York Islanders fan. The Rangers and Devils—both hated rivals—had recently captured Stanley Cups in back-to-back seasons. The Islanders hadn't returned to the Stanley Cup Finals since 1984, which was the year after the last of four consecutive silver chalices for the franchise. Al Arbour, who coached those cup-winning teams, had ended his second tour of duty with the Islanders in 1994. Lorne Henning, his replacement, lasted one season. In 1995, coach Mike Milbury took over a team that had missed the playoffs in four of the previous seven seasons and whose best player was named "Ziggy." Clearly, the Islanders needed to change their karma, so they decided to change their colors and logo. It ended up being a fashion disaster. We're talking "Bjork wearing that swan dress to the Oscars" kind of disaster.

The new logo was supposed to honor the heritage of Long Island, New York, as a fishing region. It depicted a white-bearded gentleman in a blue rain slicker and matching cap, gripping a hockey stick where his fishing rod would be. He looked sort of angry, like a cod just snagged his favorite lure. He also was the spitting image of the Gorton's Fisherman frozen-food logo. More on that later. The team's traditional blue-and-orange color scheme was given a third color—minty green. The team of Mike Bossy and Bryan Trottier now looked like a skating advertisement for Aquafresh toothpaste.

Islanders fans despised the change, ignoring racks of new sweaters and opting to keep their old jerseys (which weren't exactly on the cutting edge of good taste to begin with). Opposing fans, especially in Madison Square Garden, serenaded the Isles with chants of "fish sticks!" in honor of their new mascot.

To their credit, the Islanders were willing to admit a one-year lapse in good judgment and revert back to the traditional jerseys. But the team missed a filing deadline for uniform changes in the National Hockey League and couldn't sink the "fisherman" logo for the team's 25th anniversary season in 1996. Just to rub it in, the league did allow the team to wear its old jerseys as an "alternative" jersey, just so fans could see how crappy the new logo really was.

Roller Hockey International

A Dumber Version
of Roller Derby

THE FIRST warning sign about Roller Hockey International, which spun its wheels from 1992 to about 1999, was the league's definition of *international*. Its first season featured three franchises in Canada, and the rest were in the United States. I've had coffee creamers that were more international than that.

Then there were team names that were about as marketable as an *E. coli* burger. The Orlando Rollergators? The Atlanta Fire Ants? The Toronto Planets? The Calgary Radz? These are the kinds of nicknames that they use in the movies when professional teams refuse to share their copyrights.

In theory, the RHI had potential. Rollerblades were all the rage among American teens, and the National Hockey League was in the midst of expanding to the western and southern United States. Arenas were empty for most of the summer (this was before the juggernaut that is the WNBA), and all RHI needed was a rink-sized slab of concrete (*check!*), owners such as Jerry Buss and Mark Messier to invest (*check!*), and scores of minor-league and washed-up NHL players willing to strap on blades of plastic (*check!* although it breaks my heart to call Tiger Williams and Bryan Trottier washed-up, even though they were).

Roller Hockey International was yet another inspiration from sports promoter Dennis Murphy. He previously cofounded the American Basketball Association and the World Hockey Association, two leagues that scared the hell out of their more-established rivals. The NBA and NHL gobbled up four franchises apiece when the ABA and WHA finally folded.

As for Murphy's World Team Tennis organization . . . how can you not love a league that featured Chris Evert and a franchise called the Hawaii Leis?

Those leagues had their virtues; alas, RHI did not. The games were played four-on-four with rules against physical play, which opened up the floodgates for scoring. Games averaged 100 shots on goal and 16.7 goals scored. It was a clear case of catering to the "casual" fan and turning off dedicated sports fanatics who like a little defense mixed in with their offense. Also, players had these slightly baggy warm-up pants as part of their uniforms, giving the league a "wearing my daddy's clothes" sort of countenance.

Have I mentioned that RHI openly embraced socialism? Every player on a team was paid the same wage regardless of merit. The deeper the team advanced into the playoffs, the more money that was added to the team's coffer, to be shared equally. If roller hockey had been around in his day, Stalin would have commissioned the Moscow Commiez in a millisecond. The RHI also alienated some of its most successful franchises (including Minnesota and Pittsburgh) by spreading their league fees to unstable teams that couldn't meet their financial obligations.

The biggest blow to the fledgling league was overexpansion. Twelve teams in 1993 became 24 by 1994. From 1992 to 1999, the RHI saw 41 different teams, from the Anaheim Bullfrogs to the Vancouver Voodoo; since 1927, the NHL has seen only 54.

By 1999, Roller Hockey International—which drew 1.3 million fans in its second season—was down to eight teams, half of which averaged less than 1,000 fans per game. The league had gone several years without a national television contract. It finally collapsed, folding four more teams, including league champion St. Louis.

Orlando Rollergators, we hardly knew ye . . .

Drafting a Player Who Doesn't Exist
The Buffalo Sabres Get Creative

I N 1974, competition for top young talent between the National Hockey League and the upstart World Hockey Association was intense. The WHA was in its third year of operation and had begun signing Canadian junior-league players that were too young to be drafted by the NHL (which required draftees to be at least 20 years old). With prospects such as defenseman Mark Howe beginning to jump to the WHA with some frequency, the NHL in 1974 successfully lobbied to drop the age requirement for its first two rounds—a huge policy change for the stodgy league.

To further counter its rival, the NHL moved its 1974 entry draft two days before the WHA's to have a window of exclusivity to sign selected players. The NHL was so obsessed with hoarding junior hockey's top prospects that it decided to hold the 1974 draft as a secret conference call from league head-quarters in Montreal.

This would prove to be quite foolish, as the draft selections took longer than usual, pushing the final picks to within hours of the WHA's draft. The tedious process so angered Buffalo Sabres general manager George "Punch"

Imlach that the former Maple Leafs coach decided to take out his frustrations in an incredibly creative but ultimately unseemly manner. In the 11th round of the 1974 NHL draft, with the 183rd pick, Imlach selected Taro Tsujimoto of the Tokyo Katanas in the "Japanese league." He claimed Tsujimoto was a star center for the team. The league validated the selection without a second thought, and rival GMs wondered who this mysterious player was.

Weeks later, Imlach came clean. There were no Tokyo Katanas—in fact, "katanas" is Japanese for "sabres"—and there was no Taro Tsujimoto either. The Far East phenom was born out of Imlach's exasperation with the draft process. One story had Imlach simply picking Tsujimoto's name out of a phonebook; another claimed that Buffalo owner Seymour Knox III had been served by a waiter with that name while dining in a Japanese restaurant the evening before the draft.

The NHL wiped "Taro Tsujimoto" from its official draft records, referring to Imlach's 1974 selection simply as "invalid claim."

The WHA eventually folded in 1979.

No word on the fate of the fabled "Japanese league."

Attack of the Third Jerseys
Making a Quick Buck
through Fashion Disasters

*F*LASHBULBS *illuminate a small auditorium as paparazzi, celebrities, and industry icons crowd around a 30-foot platform.*

Hello everyone, and welcome to the fabulous runways of Milan, where we're taking a trip down Fashion Lane into the spectacular world of alternative sports apparel! At some point in the mid-1990s, professional sports owners all came to the same conclusion: they wanted to make more money . . . like, really fast. Rather than upset the clothing conservatives by radically changing their players' wardrobes, they had the most revolutionary stroke of fashion genius since the zipper: enter, the third jersey!

Alternative uniforms started showing up in the American League back in 1994, with teams such as Toronto, Oakland, and the Chicago White Sox offering solid-colored jerseys as part of their ensemble. The following season, the NHL began its lucrative third-jersey program, followed by the NBA late in the decade and the NFL in 2002. Football helped kick-start the third-jersey craze when it allowed teams to wear retro jerseys in the NFL's 75th anniversary season, in 1994; by 2003, teams such as the Redskins and Dolphins had officially made their retro apparel their alternate uniforms.

Shhh . . . the models are about to hit the runway! It's the debut of our fall collection: the worst third jerseys in sports history!

Pounding techno music begins as several men in sports jerseys mull around in the back of the runway. One of them approaches the stage.

Here's Paul Kariya of the Mighty Ducks of Anaheim, strutting in their 1995–1996 alternate sweater. C'mon, Paul, show us sexy! It wasn't bad enough that the team was named after some silly kids' movie; these paid professionals now had to skate around in a jersey that featured a cartoon-duck superhero appearing to burst forth from their own kidneys! The alternate logo certainly had class—as in, it looked like it had been designed by Mrs. McGinley's kindergarten class.

Speaking of pucks, here comes the Janet Jones of hockey, Mr. Wayne Gretzky, in the Los Angeles Kings' third jersey from 1996. It's a real goth look: a pure white sweater with a dark gray swirl, looking a bit like a cadaverous sundae. The pale, purple-bearded face of a king is over the left breast, resembling a ZZ Top guitarist rescued hours after falling through a frozen lake. Like the Ducks' third jersey, this, too, lasted but one season.

Ah, yes! It's time for supermodel Antoine Walker of the Dallas Mavericks, sporting a shimmery silver alternate road jersey from 2003. Talk about your fashion disasters: the Mavericks wore these duds for one game and received so much ridicule that the team put them back in mothballs forever! Flamboyant Dallas owner Mark Cuban told *USA Today* that "the uniforms didn't look on the court like we expected them to." Guess he didn't expect them to look like futuristic garbage bags!

Another sweater from "Big D!" Here's cheekbones-straight-from-heaven Mike Modano with the 2003 Dallas Stars' third jersey. Say, what's that on the front? As the team officially called the logo, "a constellation of individual stars aligning to form an unstoppable force of nature." Then again, it also sort of looks like . . . a diagram of the female reproductive system? Gross! Hey, here's some breaking news: You're a hockey team! Are ovaries supposed to be intimidating?

Time for our final model, ingénue Ryan Smyth of the Edmonton Oilers. This team has truly one of the richest traditions in the NHL, with names such as Gretzky, Messier, Fuhr, Coffey, and Kurri having proudly worn the Edmonton crest. So what did it do in 2001? The Oilers introduced the male precursor to the Dallas Stars' fallopian folly. Comic book artist Todd McFarlane designed the team's alternate logo, which featured a giant drop of oil encased in some sort of rocky sprocket. Whatever it was, it looked like a sperm sample provided by the Thing from the *Fantastic Four*.

That ends our little walk-spin-walk down memory lane, looking at the crappiest couture in the history of third jerseys. Snaps to all of our models, and here's hoping for further advancements in corrective eye surgery for the designers.

OLYMPIC
ABOMINATIONS

Awarding the Olympics to the Kaiser

International Olympic Committee Misjudges the Healing Power of the High Jump

NEXT TIME you see the Olympic torch bounding through your town, be sure to find the nearest Nazi and give him your heartfelt appreciation.

Yep . . . just like public broadcasting and sarin gas, the torch relay was invented by a German and popularized by Adolf Hitler. Der Führer celebrated the torch relay as a symbol of national power during the 1936 Summer Olympics, which had been awarded to Germany two years before his Nazi party came to power in 1933. The United States nearly boycotted the Berlin Games but decided to look past racism and anti-Semitism in the spirit of athletic competition . . . paving the way for Major League Baseball to do the same in allowing Marge Schott to own the Cincinnati Reds some years later.

Despite the fact that the 1936 Summer Games were going to be a Nazi fashion show with some occasional running and jumping, the International Olympic Committee did not succumb to global pressure to move the event to another city. For the 1916 Games, however, the IOC sang a different Olympic theme.

In 1912, the IOC awarded the sixth Summer Games of the modern era to Berlin, for 1916. At first, giving Berlin the Games seemed like a brilliant idea . . . considering that Cleveland was one of the other host candidates. But what the IOC really wanted to do was exploit the Games as a political tool—in other words, to use the awarding of the Olympics as a rallying point for Germans who desired to see a political sea-change in their nation and peace in the region.

No dice. About two years later, World War I began. The IOC refused to move the Games from Berlin, hoping that the war would be over before 1916. As the battle raged on, the IOC felt pressure to shift the host city to a region that had yet to enter the war, such as the United States. But the IOC refused to budge, saying that it would not move the Games unless Germany requested that it do so.

By 1915, the war had progressed to the point that it was obvious that Berlin could not host the Olympics. The decision was finally made to cancel the Summer Games for the first time in the modern era. Belgium was selected as the next host for the 1920 Games as sort of a "Sorry Germany Invaded Your Ass in 1914" consolation from the IOC. (Germany, Austria, Bulgaria, and Hungary were banned from participating in the 1920 event, which was held in Antwerp.)

Unfortunately, the IOC didn't learn from its 1916 debacle. Again seeking to effect change, it awarded the 1980 Summer Games to communist Russia; 65 nations, including the United States, boycotted the event.

Olympic Snowboarding
Dude . . . Seriously?

*O*N OCCASION *in this book, it becomes imperative to share an extraordinary point of view on a given theme. The only way to truly accomplish that is through the appointment of a guest essayist on said topic. This is one such instance.*

How's it hangin', two-planker? It's moi: clichéd snowboarding stoner dude!

Like, the Winter Games are so gnarly. Not only do dudes get to shred on some of the most bitchin' hills in, like, the entire universe, but I heard that the Olympic Village was like a snowbunny convention. Like, even the curling guys get some.

That's why I was so stoked when the International Olympic dudes accepted phat airdogging as an official event for the 1998 Games in Noggin Nose, Japan. They decided to have a wicked halfpipe battle and also a giant slalom, where me and the boys could totally shred some wicked backcountry. Just think about it: a glorified demonstration sport, populated by adrenaline junkies and recreational drug users, is given the same honored place on an Olympic podium as Sonja Henie. Sweet!

Well, those first Olympics kinda sucked for 'boarding. Austrian snowboarder Martin Freinademetz had his Olympic card pulled after a wild hotel party he hosted got really, really wild, causing $4,000 in damages. But the biggest bummer was when Canada's Ross Rebagliati—our first-ever gold medalist in the giant slalom—had his medal taken away after he tested positive for getting wonked on the stinkweed. The dude had a great excuse, though: he said it was second-hand smoke. Why didn't he just trot out the poppy seed defense?

Ross got his medal back because the IOC didn't actually have an agreement with the International Ski Federation that grandpa's magic eye medicine should be treated as a banned substance. But you know they put it on the list ASAP, dude.

In 2002, snowboarding took off like a hucker on a halfpipe. Little dudes and dudettes watched the Salt Lake City Games in record numbers, as the Olympics inched ever closer to becoming the X-Games. Move over figure skating: no one cares about a triple axel when you can watch a McTwist into a frontside seven with an Indy grab into a 360 mute instead, bee-otches!

Now, if you'll excuse me, I'm supposed to go "hang out" with some teammates, watch *Fantasia* for the 3,000th time, and argue for several hours about whether it's actually the snow that's riding us. Peace . . .

Reebok's "Dan and Dave"
Did Hype Harm American Track?

IN THE EARLY 1990s, Reebok was best known for two things: being the athletic shoemaker without the services of Michael Jordan and inventing the Reebok Pump—a sneaker that enabled its wearer to add or subtract air with a button on the tongue of the shoe in order to create a better fit. (The pump also was popular among obsessive-compulsives and trendy bandwagoneers that would buy a sneaker made of goat feces if the commercials were compelling enough.)

As the 1992 Summer Olympics in Barcelona approached, Reebok saw a golden opportunity in 25-year-old American decathlete Dan O'Brien. Handsome and personable, O'Brien was the reigning world champion in the grueling 10-event gauntlet and appeared to be a sure thing to make the Summer Games and battle for the gold medal.

But that wasn't enough for Reebok, which decided what O'Brien really needed was a rival whom it could market as his foil. Enter Dave Johnson, a 29-year-old decathlete who competed in the 1988 Summer Games. Despite the fact that Johnson had injured his knee and did not compete in the 1991 world championships, Reebok paired him with O'Brien in a $25 million, eight-month long advertising campaign that asked, "Who is the world's greatest athlete: Dan or Dave? To be settled in Barcelona."

Early on in the July 1992 U.S. Olympic track trials in New Orleans, the answer appeared to be Dan. His lead heading into the pole vault was so large that he entered the event looking to break the world record for points in the decathlon. Losing the title—or missing the Olympic cut—was far from anyone's imagination.

He began with a height of 15 feet, 9 inches—an overconfident decision by his coaches, who expected that their star would easily score in the event. O'Brien's first vault was a somersault below the bar. His second attempt saw him land on the bar. His third saw him miss badly, failing to even reach the apex of his vault. After the event, O'Brien learned the appalling news: he could not crack the top three and would not be joining his rival Johnson as a competitor in Barcelona.

Reebok was sent reeling. It pulled its "Dan and Dave" ads from NBC during the Olympic trials, substituting ones with "Rocket" Raghib Ismail and Roger Clemens. The multimillion dollar campaign that pondered the identity of the greatest athlete in the world was down to two options: Dave Johnson or none of the above. Continuing Reebok's red-faced year, the answer turned out to be the latter. Johnson, considered the favorite for gold in the decathlon, could only manage the bronze in Barcelona.

Reebok sold a lot of shoes thanks to Dan and Dave. But what did the added pressure do to hinder two of American track and field's greatest stars? O'Brien said that he couldn't remember a day when he didn't clear 15-9 in practice, yet he failed to do so in the Olympic trials. He admitted to thinking about the fate of the marketing campaign before his final miss and battled alcoholism after failing to make the Olympic cut. Johnson broke a bone in his foot training in anticipation of the Summer Games and missed out on the gold in what would be his final Olympics.

Minus the Reebok hype, O'Brien broke an eight-year-old world record for points in the decathlon one month after the 1992 Olympics. In the Atlanta Summer Games in 1996, again without the intense promotion of four years earlier, O'Brien became the first American since Bruce Jenner to win gold in the decathlon.

Clubbing Nancy Kerrigan
Whyyyyy!? Whyyyyy!? Whyyyyy . . . Us?

IT WAS January 6, 1994, and here's what we knew: figure skater Nancy Kerrigan—of the 1992 bronze medal and the enormous teeth—had been walloped on the right knee while in Detroit training for the Winter Olympics by what witnesses described as a 6-feet-2 white male. It was the second time in about eight months that a female athlete had been attacked, as Monica Seles was stabbed in Germany by a crazed Steffi Graff fan. Things had gotten so out of hand that former U.S. figure skating champion Tonya Harding told the *Washington Post* that she had started employing a bodyguard service for her protection.

And what a bodyguard service it was! Not only did 26-year-old Shawn Eric Eckardt protect Harding, he even adopted a Bush doctrine–esque method of preventive strikes against her enemies!

Eckardt served as a go-between for Harding's ex-husband Jeff Gillooly and a thug-about-town named Shane Stant, who actually executed the attack on Kerrigan. Eckardt—a 350-pound lunkhead—wanted to kill Kerrigan, according to Stant's FBI interview transcript. Derrick Smith, who would serve as the getaway driver for the scheme, nixed that idea and suggested that (just like Kobra Kai dojo preaches) they go for the leg. Gillooly said the hit would be financed through figure-skating sponsorship money provided to Harding by George Steinbrenner (in case you were having trouble mustering even more disdain for the New York Yankees).

Within eight days of the attack, Eckardt, Stant, and Smith had all been arrested. Gillooly was arrested a few days later, eventually pleading guilty to one count of racketeering. He implicated Harding in the plot after it became apparent to him that she was going to throw him under the bus as the mastermind of the attack.

As for Tonya—sweet, sweet Tonya—she made the U.S. women's figure skating team and competed in Norway's Winter Games. Wearing a plum-colored unitard that made her look like a pirouetting bruise, Harding nearly missed her performance, coming out of the locker room with just 21 seconds left on the clock. She missed her first jump and began to openly weep. Harding skated over to the referee and explained that one of her laces had broken during warm-ups. The referee allowed her a second chance at the routine, and later that night Harding skated well enough to place eighth overall. Kerrigan settled for the silver after the judges awarded the gold to 16-year-old Ukrainian Oksana Baiul—who once crashed a Mercedes into a tree but never hired a man-mountain to cripple a fellow skater.

Two weeks after her Olympic debacle, Harding arranged a bargain with police in which she pled guilty to hindering the investigation of the Kerrigan assault. Although evidence, and the rest of the conspirators, pointed to Harding's having played a role in organizing the attack, she was now safe from further prosecution. In exchange, she paid a number of financial penalties and was forced to surrender her membership in the U.S. Figure Skating Association. Adding insult to indignity, the USFSA stripped Harding of her 1994 national championship a few months later.

Ah, but Tonya's career continued to spiral around the bowl. A sex tape that she and Gillooly made on their honeymoon was "leaked," and Tonya proved to be the most unattractive thing in a wedding dress this side of Dennis Rodman. In 2000, she assaulted her new boyfriend with a hubcap, splitting his lip. That landed her in jail for three days.

A couple of alcohol-related problems with the law preceded what would be her next great stab at stardom: FOX's *Celebrity Boxing* special, in which Tonya was scheduled to fight fellow white-trash goddess Amy "Long Island Lolita" Fisher. But Fisher's parole board wouldn't allow her to fight, and Bill Clinton accuser Paula Jones stepped in to replace her. Every time Harding tried to punch her, Jones spun away from the pain . . . much like yours truly did the first time that I saw Paula Jones in a *Penthouse* pictorial.

After brief dalliances with bad singing and even worse acting, Harding seems to have settled on a "foxy boxing" sideshow of a career—which means that in just over a decade, she went from being the first American women's skater to successfully hit a triple axel in a championship competition to the female version of Butterbean.

Great career move, that hit on Kerrigan, wasn't it?

AWFUL INNOVATIONS

PART 11

The World Bodybuilding Federation

Muscles, Self-Tanner, and Complete Disaster

ASSUMING THAT the XFL was the nadir of Vincent K. McMahon's career as a promoter is an insult to the World Bodybuilding Federation (as well as to the wrestling plumber, the wrestling NASCAR driver, the wrestling garbage man, the wrestling voodoo priest whose magic hex made the Ultimate Warrior vomit some sort of green goo live on camera, something called Bastian Booger, something else called the Gobbledygooker, and every other rotten wrestling gimmick Vinnie Mac invented).

By the early 1990s, as president of the World Wrestling Federation, McMahon had learned a lesson or two about conquering industries filled with muscle-bound lunkheads. For example,

1. Mock, raid, and destroy your competition by any means necessary.
2. Pay-per-view equals money-in-pockets.
3. Come as close to being a modern-day P. T. Barnum as you can without having to actually put your head in a lion's mouth.

In 1990, McMahon—a weightlifting aficionado—had denied that he was interested in creating a WWF-like bodybuilding league that would compete with the well-established International Federation of Bodybuilders. He insisted that his interest was simply to publish a new magazine about weight training. Then, after the conclusion of the IFBB's signature "Mr. Olympia" event in Chicago that year, McMahon and his "magazine" staff stunned the crowd by revealing their true intentions. They handed out flyers heralding the dawn of the World Bodybuilding Federation as veteran bodybuilder turned WBF director of talent development Tom Platz took to the stage and proclaimed that the fed would "kick the IFBB's ass!"

In January 1991, McMahon held a press conference at the Plaza in New York City to unveil his first dozen or so WBF superstars. His plan was simple: turn these sculpted, muscle-bound specimens into stars the magnitude of his other sculpted, muscle-bound specimens in the WWF. (Judging from the unnatural enormity of some of the physiques, one might assume that it was "by any chemical means necessary.") McMahon applied the formula for success that he used in professional wrestling, issuing different personas and nicknames to the bodybuilders (the "Giant Killer," the "Phoenix"), scheduling a pay-per-view championship event at the Trump Taj Mahal in June 1991, and hosting a WBF exclusive weekly cable television show called *WBF Bodystars*, which profiled the athletes and offered nutritional and workout tips (and featured McMahon in a flattering tank top). He even used one of his wrestlers—Lex Luger, newly acquired from rival World Championship Wrestling—as a WBF "superstar" to help attract attention. (That the WBF allowed Luger a way around the noncompete clause in the WCW contract helped, too.)

But Luger's involvement is a prime example why the WBF—and later the XFL—failed: bodybuilding fans were turned off by the wrestling machinery while wrestling fans thought that the WBF didn't offer enough grappling gimmickry to interest them either. In searching for a middle ground between the two fan bases, McMahon ended up alienating them both.

Of course, McMahon also made a more general miscalculation—that bodybuilding was popular enough to receive the kind of push that he intended to give it. His cult of wrestling fans didn't care if their athletes had perfectly toned brachioradialis or latissimus dorsi muscles; they just wanted to see a figure-four leglock, a flying elbow drop, or Doink, the evil wrestling clown. Now that's entertainment!

The WBF's darkest hour came in that first pay-per-view event, dubbed the World Bodybuilding Federation Championship. The event itself was a boring mess that didn't really seem to have a point, beyond being an excuse to listen to "Mean" Gene Okerlund and Bobby the "Brain" Heenan—the Madden and Summerall of professional wrestling—for a few hours. Fans universally ignored the broadcast, resulting in embarrassingly low buy rates around the country, especially in relation to the WWF's typical business. An Anaheim, California, cable company reported that out of its 40,000 subscribers, exactly four of them purchased the WBF event—perhaps by accident.

Nearly a year later, McMahon called his competition at the IFBB and announced that he was shutting down the magazine and the WBF. Reports stated a $15 million loss for the federation.

Drug-Testing Policies
The No. 1 Reason Why Keith Richards Learned to Play Guitar

TO SAY that drug-testing policies in professional sports are hypocritical would be an insult to any man who has openly criticized pornography as being "demeaning to women" but who has seen the Pam and Tommy tape more times than he's seen *Star Wars*.

A little recreational drug use? Enjoy your suspension, Sir Smokes-a-Lot. Yet professional athletes are somehow allowed to ingest more chemical strength enhancement than the manimals on the isle of Dr. Moreau. Considering how often they've chosen to look the other way when it comes to steroids, it's laughable that professional sports attempt to claim the moral high ground with their drug-testing policies. They claim that they're trying to keep their athletes off recreational drugs because they serve as "role models" for young fans. Are these child advocates the same ones that begin championship games at 9:00 PM on a school night?

Unlike Charles Barkley, I think that athletes are role models, as are singers, musicians, actors, actresses, and teachers. But when it comes to recreational drugs—marijuana, cocaine, hallucinogens, what have you—why are athletes held to a standard higher than that of performers in the entertainment industry? How many parents overlooked extreme violence in letting their kids watch the R-rated *Matrix* films, even though star Keanu Reeves admitted to *Vanity Fair* magazine in 2001 that he's had some "*really* wonderful experiences" with illegal drugs? How many parents allow their kids to buy a CD without demanding to see the results of the band's urinalysis test? Hell, I never heard anyone complain that Belushi was "just too coked up" when he was doing the Samurai Chef on *SNL* back in 1975. Doesn't it bother anyone that we live in a society that mandates random drug tests for athletes but not for the majority of schoolteachers?

Maybe you believe that athletes should be prohibited from smoking a joint on an off day. That's cool. But you still have to admit that there are glaring inconsistencies in the drug-testing policies for professional sports. The NFL, for example, will dole out a four-game suspension to a player after his third positive test for a nonsteroid drug. Compare that with its substance abuse policy for referees, who aren't allowed to consume a single alcoholic drink for 36 hours before a game. Who is more likely to be a role model for young fans: Randy Moss or Ed Hochuli?

Look at the difference between the NBA and the NHL, whose teams share an arena but little else when it comes to drug testing. The NBA tests rookies up to four times a season but tests veteran players only once, randomly, during training camp. The NHL doesn't test any player that isn't already in the league's substance-abuse aftercare program. So unless you're fresh out of a college dorm room or already on dope, they really don't care what you're smoking.

Do our attitudes toward drug testing in pro sports symbolize some of the institutional biases that burden us? Do we desire strict testing in Major League

Baseball because we hold that sport to some idealized notion of Americana? Does the NBA opt for a less-stringent policy because the socioeconomic origins of many of its players increase the chances that they may use recreational drugs? And if these leagues really wanted drugs out of their locker rooms, why not bully the players' associations into one-and-done enforcement?

When it comes to drug policy, I think Will Rogers said it best: "Prohibition is better than no liquor at all."

The Black-Jersey Trend
Never Bet on Black

THERE ARE people who are what they wear. Guys in fur coats naturally have a pimp walk. Girls who start wearing dresses made of hemp will eventually lather themselves in patchouli. And then there are those dudes who throw on camouflage military pants and say stuff like "Life is a battle, and I'm a soldier who's not going out like that." Those guys scare me.

It's only natural that sports teams would want to attire their athletes in something that suggests ferocity, nobility, or several other words that end with *ity* (like *agility, invincibility, intensity, veracity* . . . meh, that might be it.) Changing uniforms can have an amazing effect on a franchise's fortunes, on and off the field. When the New Jersey Devils stopped looking like a bunch of Christmas trees on skates, they went on to win three Stanley Cups. The Denver Broncos lost four Super Bowls in their light-blue and orange jerseys; as soon as they went to those bitchin' dark-blue uniforms, they won two championships. The best case study of all was that of the Tampa Bay Buccaneers, who used to look like a team that took a collective Gatorade bath before the game. When they moved to copper and red, they won the Super Bowl. Case closed.

But by and large, teams that change their uniforms do so for one reason: to bilk more money out of their customers and ideally come up with a design that becomes a fashion trend among out-of-town fans. The Chicago White Sox sold gear in and out of the Windy City when they went to black and white in 1990. That move, combined with the continued popularity of the silver-and-black Raiders paraphernalia and the blue-but-nearly-black-pinstriped Yankees uniforms, started a movement in the 1990s in which seemingly every team in organized sports added black as a primary color to its wardrobe.

There's no question that it worked for some teams, such as the Los Angeles Kings (who couldn't sell enough silver-and-black Gretzky sweaters) and the Atlanta Falcons (who returned to the black uniforms that they wore in the 1970s). But in the end, it was overkill. How can a hockey team use black in its uniforms to look like a bunch of bad asses when the Flyers, Stars, Devils, Sharks, Lightning, Blackhawks, Senators, and Sabres already do the same? The New York Knicks and Mets added black to their blue and orange uniforms; let's just say that they weren't exactly invited to Fashion Week. Then came the alternate jerseys in football, with teams such as the Eagles and the Jaguars opting for the all-black look and instead looking like mint chocolate-chip ice cream.

The most frustrating case in the black-uniform revolution? The debut of the Colorado Rockies in 1993. The Major League Baseball expansion team selected silver, purple, and black as its colors. Purple, evidently, was chosen for "purple mountain's majesty." The team's choice of silver and black was maligned by critics, including those of *Sports Illustrated*, as a blatant attempt to market its merchandise by adopting colors associated with gangs. In fact, the Rockies' *CR* hat was quickly adopted by the Crips, who claimed that it stood for "Crips Rule."

Do professional sports really need to promote that?

Tchoukball
Gesundheit!

TCHOUKBALL (pronounced "chuke-ball") is sort of the Kwanzaa of recreational athletics, but instead of being a celebration of heritage and family, it's a recently invented wussy sport that might as well be choreographed aerobics. It's not a sport born out of some centuries-old tradition. It is a hybrid created by Swiss biologist Dr. Hermann Brandt in the 1960s and then unleashed on an unsuspecting public in 1970.

Why, you may ask, did he invent an entirely new sport? Was it a hobby? Did he want to replace alpine long-distance shuffleboard as the official sport of Switzerland? Was he looking to provide ESPN with a broadcasting alternative in case high-stakes, no-limit Texas hold 'em becomes the poker equivalent of old maid one day? Actually, Brandt simply wanted to create the perfect team sport . . . for fastidious pacifists.

Seems the good doctor thought that prospective athletes were turned off by the aggressive nature of modern team sports. So he designed tchoukball so that one of the most compelling aspects of popular sports—physical confrontation—was eliminated. Teams actually don't interact during the game, even though they're on the same court and are in fact trying to defeat each other.

Confused yet? Well, what if I told you that tchoukball is a combination of handball, volleyball, jai-alai, and about 25 other less-popular sports?

It's typically played with two teams of between seven and nine players on a gymnasium basketball court. On each side of the floor is a square metal frame with a springy net in the middle. It's tilted at an angle of 55 degrees, pointed to the court. Within three meters of each frame is a forbidden zone, which players cannot enter. Offense resembles handball: three seconds and three steps before a pass, three passes before a shot. Teams score by hurling the ball—a typical handball—and bouncing it off either of the frames. If it hits the floor, that's a point; if the defense catches it on the fly, there's no point and the defense takes over possession. If the shooter doesn't hit the frame or if the ball lands in the forbidden zone, the defense gets a point.

But what's the point of defense? Opposing players are prohibited from blocking an offensive player's progress, shot, or pass. There's no defending the goal or even trying to intercept a long pass down the court. You'll find more physical contact between competitors in a game of miniature golf. The only thing that the defense does is catch the ball when it rebounds off the frame—meaning that the only differences between tchoukball defenders and a golden retriever are opposable thumbs.

Having actually seen a tchoukball game, here's how this thing plays out: Offensive players leave their feet on half their shots, flying over the forbidden zone like a bunch of junior-varsity slam-dunk competition entrants. The defense—such as it is—surrounds the forbidden-zone arch waiting for a rebound. Many of them get on their knees in preparation for a shot, making tchoukball the only sport besides arena football in which defenders appear to be literally begging for mercy.

So tchoukball isn't exactly the greatest of ideas, but it does have one benefit: it may be the first team sport specifically designed for chiraptophobics.

Slot Machines Meet
Horse Racing
The Sport of Kings Takes a Gamble

*O*N OCCASION *in this book, it becomes imperative to share an extraordinary point of view on a given theme. The only way to truly accomplish that is by appointment of a guest essayist on said topic. This is, again, one such instance.*

Hello there. I'm the Devil.

Satan, Lucifer, Beelzebub, the Beast. Please allow me to introduce myself: I'm a man of wealth and taste. I'm also responsible for the bubonic plague, the *Hindenburg*, and Hanson's "MMMBop." I've always been able to count on three surefire ways to tempt the souls of mortal men: women, power, and, above all else, sports. I mean, do you have any idea how many Villanova fans I have coming to me in exchange for that win over Georgetown back in '85?

Nothing puts a point on my pitchfork more than those deals that, on the surface, seem too good to be true but end up causing corruption and despair—like, for example, when I helped poison the sport of horse racing with massive amounts of slot machine gambling. From 1985 to 1995, attendance at horse-racing facilities had dropped 41 percent. Revenues were down.

Tracks were closing. So I began appearing in feedbags and bales of hay throughout Delaware, Iowa, Louisiana, New Mexico, West Virginia, and Rhode Island, telling track owners that installing one-armed bandits was the only way to keep their sorry little sport afloat.

They all heard me, loud and clear. Slot machines and video gambling spread like a virus, propping up decrepit facilities, bringing in millions of dollars, and pissing off politicians in neighboring states. Horse racing, that silly American institution, had been reduced to a muted television in the back of a casino. It's only a matter of time before they stop racing horses all together and just use them to cart around free booze to the gamblers.

Oh, and slots are just the start; wait 'til the full casino games come in. Who needs the daily double when you can spend the whole day doubling down at a blackjack table? Who needs the Triple Crown when you have a Crown Royal on the rocks in one hand and a pair of dice in the other?

Yes . . . I was able to disgrace a sport with hundreds of years of tradition while bankrupting hundreds of people every month with my wonderfully addictive slot machines. I just wish I could have done it all sooner: they never would have run that match race between War Admiral and Seabiscuit back in '38 if the only people at the track were a bunch of blue hairs looking for three cherries in a row.

Now, if you'll excuse me, I have rush hour in Washington, D.C., to tend to . . .

FOOTBALL FUMBLES

PART 12

The Tuck Rule
First Recorded Instance of Pirates Getting Raped, Pillaged

NEW ENGLAND Patriots quarterback Tom Brady was addressing the media, and, for some reason, he was dressed like an 18th-century boot-black with a silly gray chauffeur's hat and an unzipped leather jacket. It was January 21, 2002, and it was still snowing on the very field where the Patriots had just won an overtime AFC divisional playoff game against visiting Oakland, 16–13. In fielding what was an inevitable question, Brady got this enormous smirk on his face, looking like Matt Damon with 25 extra teeth.

"Were you throwing the ball?" the reporter asked.

Brady turned to his left. "Yeah, I was throwing the ball."

If words could wink, his would have.

"I was gonna throw it, and he hit me as I was throwin' it," Brady said as he glanced down at the microphone bank in front of him, perhaps stifling a laugh. The look on the quarterback's face was similar to that of a child as his or her mother holds an empty cookie jar: "But mommy, maybe somebody came in and *stole* the last cookie . . ."

Brady smiled and looked back at the reporters. "How do you like that [explanation]?" he asked with a knowing shrug of his shoulders that seemed to scream, "I don't know what happened and I don't care what happened! How 'bout dem apples, bee-otch?"

Meanwhile, Raiders defensive back Charles Woodson—who blitzed Brady and forced what was initially ruled a fumble—found himself surrounded by the media in his interview room. His demeanor was slightly less sunny than Brady's: "It's some bullshit. You know . . . that's exactly how I feel. It's a bull-shit call. Never should have been overturned. The guy, you know, he pumped the ball, brung it back down. Maybe he wanted to bring it back up and throw again, but I hit him before he had a chance to do that. The ball came out. Game over."

What was the world like before football fans discovered the tuck rule on that snowy evening in Foxboro? Honestly, I don't remember. Maybe we trusted the referees a little more. Maybe we hoped that instant replay would counteract the idiotic rules that defy logic on the field during critical moments of the game. Maybe we all assumed that this world was one in which a fumble was a fumble, one that didn't need officials schooled in the nuance of interpretive dance to figure out what the hell the quarterback was "intending" to do.

The tuck rule, in part, reads that "any intentional forward movement of [the quarterback's] arm starts a forward pass . . . even if the player loses possession of the ball as he is attempting to tuck it back toward his body." So, in other words, if at any time the hand with the ball is coming forward and the ball comes loose, it's an incomplete pass—that is, unless the quarterback gets the ball back to his body, then it's a fumble . . . which, if you think about, is completely stupid. It basically means that everything from a pump fake to an involuntary jerk of the arm during a scramble could be construed as an attempted pass. Why not just ban quarterback fumbles entirely while you're at it?

Much-maligned referee Walt Coleman was lauded by some as having correctly applied the tuck rule in the Raiders-Patriots game in 2002. I never had a problem with the guy. To me, he's no different from a cop who busts you for smoking a joint in your basement—if you don't think it's fair, don't blame the enforcement, blame the law.

But tuck rule or no tuck rule, we all know that history had already been written: New England was going to win that game, the AFC title game, and then Super Bowl XXXVI. As if the boys in Washington weren't going to fix it so that a team called the Patriots wins the first post–September 11 championship . . .

I have a friend who's a big Patriots fan. He's seen New England win multiple Super Bowls, and now he's even seen his beloved Red Sox break a near-century-long "curse." Yet bring up the tuck rule game and call the victory—and thus, the Super Bowl trophy—a slightly tainted one, and that Bostonian swagger is reduced to a series of unprintable expletives that can be summarized as "Shut up, you stupid jealous Jets fan."

Which, of course, I am . . .

College Bowl Sponsorship
Presented by Tampax

BACK IN the day, all that you needed to separate a college bowl from any old regular season contest was a fruit bowl and an atlas. There was the Cherry Bowl, the Raisin Bowl, and the Salad Bowl. There was the Dixie Bowl, the California Bowl, and the Garden State Bowl.

In a way, bowl sponsorship had been around for decades before the preposterous explosion of naming-rights deals in the 1990s. The Citrus Bowl, for example, was actually the Florida Citrus Bowl; the Florida Department of Citrus took over the Tangerine Bowl in 1983 and rechristened it as a promotional vehicle. The Hall of Fame Bowl existed to raise funds for the College Football Hall of Fame. The John Hancock Bowl was named for the insurance company, not the signer of the Declaration of Independence.

But around 1990, things got out of hand. Corporate names became affixed to the games that they sponsored. Whatever media companies had their hands in the bowl's coffer purposefully referred to the game by its full title, forcing *SportsCenter* talking heads to navigate around names like the "Homepoint.com Music City Bowl."

In many cases, sponsorship eliminated tradition, as bowl names of yore were replaced by the companies that sponsored them. (Goodbye Mobile Bowl;

hello, GMAC Bowl.) Now, bowl sponsorship has turned what was once a proud achievement for a college football player into a confounding mishmash of here-today-gone-tomorrow sponsors. I pity the poor father who has to explain to his son that he once played in the Blockbuster Bowl before it was called the Carquest Auto Parts Bowl or the MicronPC Bowl or the Tangerine Bowl (part deux) or the Champs Sports Bowl.

Can you match the following college bowl games with their one-time sponsors?

1. Holiday Bowl	A. Chick-fil-A
2. Citrus Bowl	B. Tostitos
3. Las Vegas Bowl	C. Crucial.com
4. Peach Bowl	D. Culligan
5. Fiesta Bowl	E. MasterCard
6. Alamo Bowl	F. Ourhouse.com
7. Humanitarian Bowl	G. Pioneer PureVision

ANSWERS: *1D, 2F, 3G, 4A, 5B, 6E , 7C*

NFL Crowd-Noise Rule

Shhhhh . . . Someone's Playing Professional Football

HOW IMPORTANT is home-field advantage in the National Football League? It's the reason why several teams have banners hanging in their stadiums honoring the fans as the "12th man." Seventy thousand people screaming their beer-soaked lungs out can turn an opposing offense into a chaotic mess while serving as the ultimate motivator for the home-team defense.

Because they can affect the outcome of the game, fans are expected to provide all the enthusiasm and volume they can muster for four quarters. The PA announcer asks for it. (*Hey fans . . . it's fooooooourth down!*) The scoreboard and stadium music encourage it. Hell, if you're not up on your chair and bellowing like a mental patient during a goal-line stand, it's guaranteed that some guy with a painted face is going to bash you on the skull with his hardhat until you are.

Yet with all that pressure on fans to make as much noise as they can, the NFL actually prohibits them from making too much of it. In one of the preeminent killjoy moves in sports history, the NFL's Competition Committee created a "crowd noise" rule in the late 1980s in response to deafening home fields such as the Kingdome in Seattle. Under the rule, an opposing player could ask the referee to do something about the "excessive" crowd noise that was hindering the effectiveness of his team's audibles. The officials would then make an announcement to the crowd, asking for a reasonable decrease in volume. This request would inevitably lead to an immediate increase in amplification—in the form of booing, hissing, and creative expletives—which would leave the referee no choice but to take away a timeout from the home team or levy a five-yard penalty if the home team is out of timeouts.

Basically, the rule is a delay-of-game call, even though one team is ready to play and the other team would be ready if it wasn't so damn preoccupied with what the paying customers are saying.

The crowd-noise rule remains one of those quirky laws that's on the books but is rarely enforced, like those city ordinances from 1845 that ban cats from drinking whiskey on a Thursday while wearing a fisherman's hat. The only time that enforcement of the rule is even considered is when teams are accused of artificially pumping up the volume, such as when music or prerecorded cheering is broadcast after the visiting team breaks an offensive huddle.

This rule is incongruous on three levels. First, who the hell cares what a team does to enhance its home-field advantage? Anything short of having the cheerleaders perform a defensive endzone burlesque show during a fourth-and-goal situation should be legal. Second, why would the NFL do anything to muzzle its most loyal customers? Garish volume is a problem that most professional sports would love to have; why not ship some of that excess noise over to Major League Baseball so that games in May don't sound like the smoking lounge in the basement of a funeral home? Finally, for an all-American outfit like the NFL, could it possibly have a more unpatriotic statute on the books? Not only does the crowd-noise rule violate the fans' constitutional protection against abridgement of their freedom of speech, but it also violates their right to peacefully assemble as well. It completely strips away the right of five fat guys to wear pig snouts and women's dresses and scream like they're skydiving without a parachute for three hours. That's half of the first amendment, for God's sake!

I can hear our forefathers weeping now . . .

Canadian Football
Invades America
A Bad-Tasting Import

MICHAEL J. FOX. Shania Twain. John Candy, Dan Aykroyd, Rick Moranis, and Martin Short. The Barenaked Ladies. The Expos, Nordiques, Jets, Grizzlies, and Wayne Gretzky.

America has pilfered plenty from its friends to the *nord*. In fact, the only things we haven't taken from Canada are the Tragically Hip and universal health care. I imagine that plenty of Canucks have spent many a night in their igloos, the smell of back bacon in the air, gulping their Molsons and plotting their revenge by drawing up invasion plans with hockey sticks in the snow— until, of course, someone spots a moose and everybody grabs his RCMP billy club to begin the great white hunt.

In 1994, Canada revealed its maniacal scheme to finally even the score against its border-hogging, *Kids in the Hall*–scorning chums to the south: spreading the scourge of the Canadian Football League and its third-down punts to unsuspecting American cities.

Sacramento was the first guinea pig. Basically, the city's World League of American Football team—the Surge—morphed into the Sacramento Gold

Miners of the CFL. The Miners were meant to be one of two U.S. teams in the CFL's first wave of American expansion. But San Antonio's franchise never got off the ground, forcing Sacramento to exist without any marketing help from the CFL to get fans to pay for games against teams named the Alouettes and the Argonauts. On top of that, the Miners played in some craphole called Hornet Field, which housed a delightful array of port-o-potties (or, for our Canadian friends, an array of "oot-houses") in place of actual bathroom facilities. After two years of poorly attended games, Sacramento relocated to (where else?) San Antonio, to become the Texans for one season.

The three-year CFL infestation into the United States saw short-lived franchises in Birmingham; Memphis (the Mad Dogs, owned by FedEx's Fred Smith, whose field wasn't even CFL-regulation length); Shreveport (the Pirates, who called the second floor of the Louisiana State Fair's livestock barn "home" during their first training camp); and the Las Vegas Posse.

Perhaps one of the most pathetic franchises in the history of organized sports, the Posse's only claim to fame was its July 8, 1994, win over Sacramento in the first meeting between American CFL teams. The rest of the team's history was soaked in infamy. There was the time that the Posse's pregame entertainment sang the Canadian national anthem to the tune of "O Christmas Tree." There was the team's gaggle of XFL-ish scantly clad cheerleaders, who were sometimes sent behind the opposing bench to distract visiting players. There was the fact that the team cut tickets to $9 apiece by the end of the season and "appeased" ripped-off season-ticket holders by giving them extra tickets to the games that they didn't even want to attend in the first place! Vegas was such a disaster that it moved its final home game 1,490 miles away—to Edmonton, where the CFL belonged.

Lack of both fan support and a major television contract killed the American experiment in 1995. To be fair, the CFL did have one tremendous success story in Baltimore. The franchise went 27–9 in two seasons and captured the Grey Cup in 1995. More important, the Stallions averaged just under 34,000 fans per game at Memorial Stadium in their two seasons, paving the way for Art Modell to steal the Browns from Cleveland and place them in Charm City. The Baltimore Ravens chased the CFL's Stallions out of town, and in 2001 the NFL team won the next best thing to the Grey Cup—something called Super Bowl XXXV.

Mixing Santa with Philly Fans
Ho, Ho, Ho . . . ly Crap

THEY'VE BEEN known to throw batteries, pennies, bags of unidentified liquid substances, and (mostly) fists at opposing fans. They've become notorious for booing their own picks in the NFL entry draft. They've even razzed a visiting player (ex-Cowboy Michael Irvin) as he lay paralyzed on the field, mock-cheering even louder when he was finally carried into the locker room on a stretcher.

But what cemented Philadelphia fans' reputation as the most amoral, loathsome collection in sports came at the expense of a certain jolly old elf. It was December 15, 1968. The Eagles were home against the Minnesota Vikings. It was a game they would lose, falling to 2–12 for the season. Over 54,000 fans crowded Franklin Field for the contest, which was played during a snowstorm.

Eagles fans had a reason to be surly beyond their team's awful record. Former Washington Redskins coach Joe Kuharich had been hired as the team's coach/GM in 1964 and produced just one winning season. He also traded quarterback Sonny Jurgensen to the Redskins for fellow signal caller Norm Snead. In 1967, Jurgensen led the league in passing; in 1968, Snead had 11 touchdowns and 21 interceptions for the Eagles.

According to *The Great Philadelphia Fan Book*, written by radio hosts Glen Macnow and Anthony Gargano, there was supposed to be a Christmas pageant at halftime of the Eagles-Vikings game. But the conditions were so bad that a float couldn't make its way around the field. Instead, a 19-year-old fan named Frank Olivo—wearing a Santa Claus suit and fake beard in the stands—was invited to run through two columns of cheerleaders on the field in celebration of Jesus's birth (or something like that).

Perhaps, as the authors suggest, this Santa was just a surrogate for Kuharich, Snead, and every other party to the Eagles' demise. Whatever the case, Philadelphia fans heartily booed this pseudo–St. Nick and pelted him with snowballs. From that moment on, the City of Brotherly Love became the City That Booed Santa.

The sports world should have learned its lesson about mingling Kris Kringle with Keystone State fans. But in 2003, Santa Claus and Philadelphia again crossed paths, although indirectly. On December 23, the New York Islanders offered a free ticket to any fan dressed in a red Santa suit, along with a trip down to the ice after the first period for a holiday pageant. Over 500 fans came dressed for the occasion, but a few had devious intentions. While on the ice, they took off their Santa duds to reveal jerseys of the hated New York Rangers. A mêlée ensued, and suddenly a three-minute publicity stunt turned into a nine-minute game delay and the lead highlight on that evening's *SportsCenter.*

After the offending Santas were cleared from the ice, the Islanders skated back out to resume play against—you guessed it—the Philadelphia Flyers.

The Premature Death of the XFL

Made Jesse Ventura into John Madden for a Season

I DO NOT KNOW, dear readers, what has provided you with a bigger shock: seeing the letters *XFL* outside of the top 25 or seeing the words *premature*, *death*, and *of* before it.

The XFL was the brainchild of World Wrestling Federation owner Vince McMahon and NBC Sports president Dick Ebersol. The league was a joint venture that could capture both post–Super Bowl football fans and the 12-to-24-year-old television audience that advertisers would give up their first borns to effectively reach. More important, the XFL was being pitched as the next mutation of the NFL, which McMahon called an "overregulated, antiseptic league."

The XFL (the *X* stood for nothing) featured a renegade rulebook that banned fair catches; required teams to run a play to score an extra point, rather than kick the ball; and featured an opening "coin flip" that had one player from each team running at each other at midfield to recover the ball—a gimmick that famously resulted in the first injury in league history on opening night.

The media condemned the XFL from its inception. Venerable political columnist George Will wrote, "The XFL will offer puerile vulgarity, vicarious danger and derivative manliness for couch potatoes." And he wrote that the week before its first game was played!

An estimated 54 million viewers tuned in on Saturday, February 3, 2001, to see the Las Vegas Outlaws shut out the New York/New Jersey Hitmen, 19–0, in the first XFL game. But the event was a microcosm of the league's problems. The quality of play wasn't good enough at first to satisfy the football fans; the lack of over-the-top violence and the league's pathetic attempts at sex appeal repelled the wrestling fans, who were promised such tantalizing minutiae as cameras inside the cheerleaders' locker rooms during halftime but instead were given double entendres by announcers like Jerry the "King" Lawler.

The media wasn't enamored either. ESPN—which didn't have a financial stake in the league and thus couldn't care less—treated the XFL like a joke, shuffling highlights to the end of *SportsCenter.* "From the ridiculous players introductions to shifting camera angles that made me dizzy, I had seen enough of the XFL by the second quarter," wrote ESPN's Mel Kiper Jr., on the network's website.

Week 2 saw the XFL's ratings slide by 50 percent. The league then went into a tailspin, the ultimate lowlight coming on St. Patrick's Day, when a game garnered just a 1.6 Nielsen rating, believed to be the lowest in prime-time history for the three major networks.

Although NBC and the WWF lost a reported $70 million, the XFL nearly had a second season. It was only when ancillary broadcasting partners UPN and TNN pulled out that McMahon said the death blow for the league was struck, three weeks after the Los Angeles Xtreme defeated the San

Francisco Demons, 38–6, in the "Million Dollar Game" for the first and only XFL title.

In the end, the quality of football had improved (give the XFL credit for correcting mistakes, for example, by allowing defensive backs to maul receivers), as did the announcing, the coverage, and even the balance between McMahon's scandalous promotion and the sensibilities of most football fans. The XFL, however, was dead.

As I said, prematurely dead. Critics who blasted the XFL in its infancy never bothered to check back and see what it had become. Fans, whose expectations had led them to think that the league should have been something that it wasn't, never stopped to appreciate what the XFL actually was.

And what was the XFL? Influential, to say the least. The same football and television executives who ridiculed the league as being sleazy and pathetic were quick to jump on the trails it blazed:

Camerawork: The XFL pioneered several types of football coverage that was later "borrowed" by competitors in the following NFL seasons: cameras in the locker room during a pregame pep talk; cameras on the sidelines, in the faces of players after big plays and coaches after big mistakes; cameras on the field and, in one very influential move, over the field—the XFL's Sky-Cam was adopted not only by ESPN's football broadcasts but also in some of its hockey coverage as well.

Audio: The XFL didn't just want a player or two with a microphone in his helmet; it wanted 20. It wanted the coaches and the cheerleaders. It wanted sideline reporters asking hard-hitting questions *during* the game. Halftime speeches by coaches were broadcast on a delay. Both the interaction and innovation of these techniques were cribbed by other networks.

Sex sells: McMahon and the XFL were the worst kind of Saturday-night date: all tease, no payoff. The cheerleaders were hyped more than the players were before the league's opening weekend. But despite a few lap dances in the stands during the game, the raunch of the XFL never reached morally outrageous proportions. McMahon let the NFL, Janet Jackson, Justin Timberlake, Terrell Owens, Nicollette Sheridan, and a wet towel handle that.

Player promotion: One of the XFL's prime offenses in the eyes of traditional football fans was the way that the players attempted to promote themselves on the field. Touchdown celebrations were encouraged. Brandon Sanders had "B. Mack" on the back of his jersey; Rod Smith famously renamed himself the ubiquitous "He Hate Me," whatever the hell that meant. Is all of this really that far removed from players' using Sharpies and cell phones after touchdowns? Or the NFL media outlets' christening defensive lineman Kabeer Gbaja-Biamila with the more marketable nickname of KGB?

OK, so the league was a disaster. This is true. But its undeniable technological and marketing influence—not to mention the conspiratorial orchestration of its demise—makes it clear that treating the XFL as DOA was a bad idea.

NFL Achievement Streaks
Ironmen Don't Need Vacation Days

THE COEN brothers' 1998 opus *The Big Lebowski* is a film filled to the gills with memorable quotes, such as when Walter (John Goodman) says to Donny (Steve Buscemi), "You have no frame of reference here, Donny. You're like a child who wanders into the middle of a movie." Imagine the history of the NFL as one big, long movie . . . like *Lord of the Rings* but with fewer Hobbits and more chop-blocking. Now imagine the NFL record book as Donny.

Frame of reference is everything when it comes to consecutive-games streaks in professional sports. Consider two historic NFL streaks by wide receivers Jerry Rice and Art Monk. Rice broke Monk's record of consecutive games with a catch, ending his streak at 274 games in September 2004 while playing with the Oakland Raiders. Monk owned the previous record at 183 games, from 1983 to 1995. Both streaks are patently bogus as "consecutive games" marks because the record book doesn't take into account the most important factor in any streak: health.

Monk missed three games with an injury in 1987 (along with a few due to the NFL players strike). In 1997, Rice blew out his knee in the 49ers' season-opening loss to Tampa Bay. He would return to catch a touchdown pass against Denver on December 15, but I'm pretty sure that he failed to garner a reception during those other 13 weeks of eating hospital food and standing on the sideline with crutches. Even the great Johnny Unitas—during his 47 consecutive games with a touchdown pass, from December 9, 1956, to December 4, 1960—missed a pair of games to injury after reaching the 21st game in the streak.

Like I said, it's all about frame of reference. The incredible streak of 2,632 consecutive games played by Cal Ripken Jr. began on May 30, 1982, and ended on September 20, 1998. As he pursued Lou Gehrig's record of 2,130, the Baltimore Orioles star never pinch-hit or pinch-ran to keep the streak alive, nor did he ever make a token appearance as a late-game defensive replacement. He played every single inning of the first 904 consecutive games. No matter how you look at it, Ripken won his battle with time and nature—the streak was legit.

Same with Joe DiMaggio's 56-game hitting streak in 1941. The New York Yankees legend's record is extraordinary; consider that DiMaggio also hit safely in both ends of seven doubleheaders during his streak and never had a game off.

So it all comes down to the not-so-subtle distinction between "consecutive games" and "consecutive games in which said player actually bothered to appear."

St. Louis Cardinals Move to Arizona
Worst Thing to Hit the Desert since *Ishtar*

"WHAT'S IN a name?" I don't know who originally said this, but I'm guessing it might have been some guy named Dick Swallow.

When the now Arizona Cardinals began as a franchise way back in 1898, they had the coolest nickname: the Chicago Normals. Think about it . . . players, upon being drafted, could don a team hat and proclaim to the world they were "proud to be Normal." (Too bad they weren't a hockey team . . . could you imagine the bad blood between the Chicago Normals and the Minnesota Wild?)

A few years after the team's inception, owner Chris O'Brien purchased some old football jerseys from the University of Chicago that had been maroon but faded over the years. O'Brien deemed the shade "Cardinal red," and the Cardinals were born.

From 1920 to 1960, the Chicago Cardinals won just two NFL championships. In 1960, the Bears had taken over Chicago; the Cardinals were bleeding money; and the NFL unanimously voted to allow them to move to St. Louis.

The next 28 years would feature just two division titles and plenty of losing seasons. By 1988, attendance had bottomed out and owner Bill Bidwell made no secret his intention to move the team out of St. Louis, especially after the city refused to build a domed stadium for his Cardinals. Suitors included Jacksonville and Baltimore, but much like Bugsy Siegel decades earlier, Bidwell looked to the desert as a land of opportunity.

The first Phoenix Cardinals game was played in 1988 in front of 51,987 fans at Sun Devil Stadium in Tempe—less than capacity by over 20,000.

Oh, but the problems didn't end there. Bidwell promptly established the highest ticket prices in the league (an average of $38 per ticket), which ticked off fans. Former season-ticket holders for the USFL's Arizona Outlaws were, because of an agreement with the city, allowed first dibs at Cardinals season tickets. That meant plenty of local high rollers whose seats weren't as good as they expected them to be, which sent lawsuits flying left and right. These incidents and others sent the Cardinals from a relocation honeymoon to matrimonial hell quicker than you can say Neil Lomax.

Then there was the team's name: the Phoenix Cardinals. State officials wanted it called the Arizona Cardinals, but Bidwell said, "The tradition of the NFL is to name the team after cities" . . . you know, like Minnesota, New England, Carolina, and Tennessee. In 1994, the team officially became the Arizona Cardinals.

Getting back to "what's in a name," the team adopted a cardinal as its mascot some years ago. It should have stuck with faded maroon—after relocation, the team's moniker became what *Sports Illustrated* has called an "ornithological oxymoron." There are no cardinals indigenous to the state, according to the Arizona Bird Committee. In fact, the only cards found in the Southwestern United States are on green felt-covered whiskey-stained tables with multicolored chips on them . . .

Using Sharp Objects for Pregame Motivation

Aren't Players Usually Worried about Getting Cut?

WIN JUST one for the Gipper.

Notre Dame's Knute Rockne made that famous speech at halftime. Judging from the actions of other football coaches, had Knute spoken before the game, it may have gone something like "Win just one for the Gipper . . . now watch me hack him with this meat cleaver."

In 1992, Mississippi State University football coach Jackie Sherrill's team was an underdog in Week 1 against the University of Texas. Sherrill saw an opportunity to educate and motivate his players in the days leading up to the game. So he asked his players whether Texas's mascot, the Longhorn, was a bull (typically defined as an uncastrated adult male of domestic cattle) or a steer (a young ox castrated before sexual maturity).

And then he had a bull named Wild Willie castrated on the practice field.

After a meeting with the university president—and during the national outcry that followed the incident—Sherrill issued a half-hearted apology:

"Even though I was not involved in the procedure that took place, I take responsibility." That didn't stop *Sports Illustrated* from christening the annual Jackie Sherrill Bonehead Award later that year.

Despite the controversy, Mississippi State had the balls to come out and beat Texas 28–10. As for Wild Willie, he was saved from the slaughterhouse—he was purchased and put out to pasture by a pair of Ole Miss fans.

Sherrill, who stepped down from the Bulldogs in 2003, has since defended the castration as a meaningful and worthy stunt. "I should have done that on the South Farm, where they do it every day, instead of on the practice field," Sherrill told the *Pittsburgh Post-Gazette*. "But I'd still do it again."

Nearly as sharp as Sherrill was the Jacksonville Jaguars' Jack Del Rio. In 2003, the first-year NFL head coach placed a tree stump and an axe in his team's locker room. It was meant to embody Del Rio's team slogan of perseverance: "Keep chopping wood."

During a 0–3 start, players took hacks at the symbolic stump to remain focused. One of those players was Pro Bowl punter Chris Hanson, who had a whack at the wood . . . and ended up chopping his non-kicking leg. He needed surgery to close the gash and missed the rest of the season for the Jaguars.

Sounds like someone put the "special" in special teams . . .

The Rooney Rule
Action? Affirmative

ONE HAS two ways of looking at the Dan Rooney rule, the 2002 bylaw regarding minority coaching candidates, named after the owner of the Pittsburgh Steelers and the chairman of the NFL's diversity committee.

First is a common critique of affirmative action in the job marketplace and academia: that minority candidates are given "special" treatment in comparison to that of white candidates because of the former's racial heritage and not because of any discernable differences in ability. Of course, that approach wouldn't be necessary but for institutional racism in some corners of the business and sports worlds—where it undoubtedly exists and continues to do so. Second is an unfortunate side effect of the affirmative action policy: tokenism, that is, interviewing minority candidates to fill an obligation—or, in more lamentable terms, a quota—even though the hiring party has already determined the person it wants to hire.

That second scenario didn't even have a chance to occur in the Rooney rule's most embarrassing moment. In 2003, Detroit Lions team president Matt Millen wanted to hire San Francisco 49ers coach Steve Mariucci as head coach. Everyone in the NFL knew that this was the case, and five minority coaching candidates actually turned down the chance to interview with the Lions because they knew that it was Mariucci's job. Nevertheless, Detroit was slapped with a $200,000 fine—the first under the Rooney rule—for not formally interviewing a minority coach for the opening.

That fine was still on the minds of the Miami Dolphins' management in 2004, when the team had its sights on Nick Saban, head coach of the 2004 conational champion LSU Tigers. Before Saban could sign on with Miami, the team had to have a Rooney rule–mandated interview with Art Shell, an African American candidate. Maximilian Schell had about the same shot as Art Shell to pass Saban on the list of candidates . . . but the Rooney rule is the Rooney rule.

By December 2004, there were five African American head coaches in the NFL. None of the hirings could directly be attributed to the Rooney rule—they were all cases of assistant coaches who paid their dues finally getting a shot . . . or in Arizona coach Dennis Green's case, a retread circling 'round the carousel again.

Is the Rooney rule worth its trouble? Perhaps not, that is, if you're like me and you think that minority hiring will increase as time passes and that the "old guard" will make way for the next generation of NFL ownership and management. Then there are other issues. Like the fact that the NCAA has a minority coaching problem that makes the NFL's look like a petty nuisance. Like the fact that the disparity is larger between blacks and whites in the hiring of cornerbacks than in that of coaches. And the fact that the Rooney rule seems geared specifically toward African American candidates—because that's the minority group that threatened legal action against the league if it didn't enact change.

But what constitutes a minority? What if I'm a team owner and I decide to interview a Latino or an Asian American candidate? In the NFL, those groups make African Americans practically look like the majority.

Hell . . . what if I interviewed a cheerleader for the job?

The Onside Kick Do-Over
When Did the NFL Become a Charity?

NFL FOOTBALL and pity make strange bedfellows. The rules of the game, at times, seem downright sadistic:

- If the quarterback gets sacked in his own end zone, not only does the defensive team get two points, it gets possession of the ball on the ensuing kickoff. Ouch!
- If a cornerback dares exhale on a wide receiver before a catchable ball reaches him, it could cost the defensive team over half the field in penalty yardage. D'oh!
- Let's say the game is tied with less than two minutes to go. The offensive team, if it's out of timeouts, is allowed one extra timeout if it has an injured player lying in agony on the field. Of course, if the clock was running when the injury timeout occurred, the ball cannot be put back in play for at least 10 seconds. And if there are only 10 seconds left in the quarter . . . game over, man. Yikes!

The NFL's merciless rulebook, however, contains one provision that appears contrary to the rest of the league's ruthless regulations. On a kickoff, the kicking team can attempt an onsides kick to try and regain possession of the ball for its offense. The kick must travel 10 yards or be touched by the receiving team to be a free ball and thus available for the kicking team to recover.

But get this: If the ball goes out of bounds on the first onside kick attempt, the kicking team is penalized only five yards and gets another attempt at the kick.

Say what? If that kickoff had gone 60 yards downfield and bounced out of bounds, the kicking team is screwed—the receiving team automatically gets the ball at the out-of-bounds spot or 30 yards from the spot of the kick. But if it's an onside kick that travels out of bounds, not only does the kicking team maintain possession, but it also gets a do-over!

In other words, a team—that at this point has played poorly enough to be losing the football game—can screw up royally, move back five yards, and get a new lease on life?

What's next? Fifth-and-goal situations? "Point-after after the point-after" attempts? What a joke.

The USFL's Trump Card
The Donald Helps Bust the NFL's Rival

INT—THE BOARDROOM, TAGLIABUE TOWER, MANHATTAN

National Football League commissioner PAUL TAGLIABUE *sits behind a long oaken conference table. On his right is* GEORGE, *a stoic and curmudgeonly lieutenant to Mr. Tagliabue; on his left is* CAROLYN, *a stoic and curmudgeonly—but in a strangely erotic way—lieutenant to Mr. Tagliabue.*

TAGLIABUE: OK, we're ready . . . send him in.

A dapper gentleman with a blue suit and matching pink tie struts into the boardroom, his hair looking like a combination of butterscotch cotton candy and a barn owl's nest. He is DONALD J. TRUMP, *a real estate mogul, reality TV star, casino magnate, and former owner of the New Jersey Generals of the United States Football League.*

TRUMP: We're going to need to make this quick. I'm buying most of 84th Street today, and then I'm going to find my next wife at the Miss Universe pageant at the fabulous Trump Taj Mahal in Atlantic City, New Jersey.

TAGLIABUE: We all know the USFL was a rival to the NFL for three seasons, from 1982 to 1985. It had a 21-game national television contract with ABC. It had plenty of smart football people behind the scenes and on the sidelines.

At one point, it had 18 teams in major football markets like New York, Philadelphia, and Chicago, along with burgeoning locales like Jacksonville. It had on-field celebrations, two-point conversions, instant replay, and a few other things the NFL was happy to steal in later seasons. It was good football and tons of fun.

CAROLYN: And then you had to go and purchase the Generals in September 1983, and the whole thing went to crap!

TRUMP: So I spent a little more money than the other owners, driving up contracts all over the league. And I might have been a little too flamboyant for my own good. But that's business, people, and I'm the best. Have you read *The Art of the Deal* or *Think like a Billionaire: Everything You Need to Know about Success, Real Estate, and Life*? If not, I have several copies under my hair . . .

GEORGE: Look, Donald: It's not the money you spent on Herschel Walker or Doug Flutie. Or the fact that you were on the back page of the *Daily News* more than the Yankees. It's the fact that you only saw the USFL as a way to get your foot in the door for the NFL through some kind of buyout or merger. You didn't think the league could make it. You thought it was a shot in the dark.

TRUMP: *(Throwing his hands in the air)* That's outrageous! Where did you get an idea like that?

GEORGE: I think it was when you told ESPN's *Outside the Lines* in 2003, "I never thought the league could make it. I thought it was a shot in the dark."

TAGLIABUE: Mr. Trump, the moment you became a part of the USFL, you were determined to force a merger between the leagues, like a next generation AFL/NFL agreement. It was the same game plan: buy up a bunch of established stars, outbid for blue-chip rookies, and set up franchises in direct competition with established NFL teams. You were the main catalyst behind trying to get the USFL to move its season from the spring to the fall to directly compete with the NFL.

TRUMP: Who wants to watch football on Easter Sunday? Easter's not about football; it's about eggs and bunnies and my incredible Easter brunch buffet at Trump Marina, prepared by my staff of world-class celebrity chefs. It's the best buffet in the entire world, and . . .

CAROLYN: *(With eyes like icy daggers)* Enough! What about that $1.7 billion antitrust suit against the NFL in 1986? You wanted to get on TV in the fall; no one wanted to put you on against the NFL; you cried foul and the league filed a monopoly lawsuit claiming that the NFL was the reason you were all $160 million in the hole.

TRUMP: Hey, we won the case!

TAGLIABUE: The jury found the NFL guilty on a single charge and didn't buy the fact that it was the reason the USFL was a financial *Titanic*. You won the case . . . and $1 in damages!

TRUMP: Which tripled to $3 under antitrust law and then, with interest, ended up being $3.76. And later, we got our court costs back from the NFL. The Donald always wins in the end!

TAGLIABUE: But the USFL lost, Mr. Trump. Lost everything. The verdict came down in July 1986, and the league's owners voted that August to cancel the season and suspend operations. Players flocked to the NFL and CFL like swallows to Capistrano. The USFL was popular, exciting, and left a legacy that influenced the NFL's own product in a significant way. But owners like you didn't want a successful competitor against the NFL—you wanted a product just good enough to annoy the league to point of merger.

Look, Mr. Trump . . . you seem like a very bright guy. And I'm sure you're going to be successful in the future. But right now, I'm sorry, Mr. Trump, but you're . . .

TRUMP: I get a yacht's worth of royalties whenever anyone says, "You're fired."

TAGLIABUE: . . . your services are no longer needed here.

TRUMP: Ohhhh . . . you're good, Tagliabue. Really good . . .

The Pro Bowl

Just Another Excuse for Pro Athletes to Get Lei-ed

IN THE hot-chicks-go-surfing movie *Blue Crush* (2002), Anne Marie (Kate Bosworth) is a Hawaiian townie that ends up hooking up with a studly young NFL quarterback (Matthew Davis), who is staying in the upscale hotel that she cleans for a living. To relay any further details of their relationship or the plot of the film would be a waste of your time, good ink, and God's patience.

As I watched the film, I figured that the most ridiculous thing in the movie would be that Anne Marie surfs in the big championship competition wearing a colored dental-floss bikini—but I was wrong. The most preposterous situation in the film was when our blonde vixen lands in Mr. Touchdown's bed for a night of passion. The next morning, the quarterback leaves nubile (and naked) Anne Marie alone in his hotel bed . . . because he has Pro Bowl practice.

C'mon . . . like they actually practice for that postseason farce?

The Pro Bowl is an excuse for NFL stars—at least the ones not feigning injury—to go to Hawaii after the season. It stopped being a legitimate all-star game in 1980, when its rotation through the league's cities ended in favor of a permanent home at Aloha Stadium in Honolulu. All-star games are migratory; the Pro Bowl is not. The NBA, NHL, and Major League Baseball all hold their all-star games midseason, surrounding them with fun skills competitions and other fanfare. The ageless argument against having the Pro Bowl after Week 9 is that the NFL doesn't want to risk injury to its star players in a meaningless exhibition—this coming from a league that now holds four weeks of preseason games, which are meaningless to everyone but the season-ticket holders who are financially obligated to attend them.

Purists like to point to the prestige of a Pro Bowl selection as a reason to respect the game. So, in theory, Dan Marino can balance his overwhelming failure to lead the Dolphins to a Super Bowl championship with his nine Pro Bowl selections. But making the Pro Bowl a bunch of times is like being an actress and snagging a dozen Golden Globe nominations: it's an honor, but it ain't no Oscar. Just like Golden Globe winners treat their awards like glorified paperweights, NFL players could care less about the Pro Bowl. In 2004, 12 players—including Randy Moss, Terrell Owens, Brett Farve, and Warren Sapp—chose not to play in the Pro Bowl because of various "injuries." How the hell can you have an all-star game without game all-stars?

The problem with the Pro Bowl is that it undermines why we have all-star games in the first place: for the fans. No one cares about the NFL from the last play of the Super Bowl until the first pick in the draft. The Pro Bowl is like a stealth fighter on a football fan's postseason radar screen, which is a shame, because the average margin of victory in those games from 1971 to 2004 is roughly 10 points.

The games are competitive, but the fans couldn't care less—and the players care even less than that.

The Bowl Championship Series
Makes HAL 9000 Look like Pollyanna

I HESITATE to place this on the list. But here it is, basically out of fear that anyone who would read this tome sans a BCS entry would put down the book, scream hellaciously, grab a torch and the nearest pitchfork, then make a beeline for my house. And with the price of giant cauldrons of boiling water for repelling rioting villagers being what it is these days, I simply cannot afford this scenario to play out (even with the six-figure advance the publisher paid me—and no, I'm not telling you where the decimal point is).

The Bowl Championship Series isn't perfect; in fact, it's a format that will consistently screw somebody out of something every single season. But so would any other possible scheme proposed to "fix" the NCAA Division I-A football playoffs.

In an effort to end the annual debate about which team is the "true" national champion, the NCAA formed the Bowl Coalition in 1992. Before the coalition, No. 1 faced No. 2 in a bowl game only nine times in the post-war era. This plan intended to increase the chances that the top two teams in the country would play in a bowl title game. It kept preexisting relationships between bowls and certain conferences while focusing on the entire season's results as well as the final poll standings.

For its first two years, consensus champions were crowned in Alabama and Florida State. In 1994, Nebraska won the national title while Penn State finished undefeated and No. 2 in the polls. Since nobody puts JoePa in a corner, the Bowl Coalition was done after three years.

Say hello to the Bowl Alliance, which involved the Fiesta, Orange, and Sugar bowls. The ACC, Big East, Big 12, and SEC (along with independent Notre Dame) agreed to participate. One bowl every year, on a rotating basis, got to match up the top two teams from those conferences. In 1995, it was No. 1 Nebraska and No. 2 Florida in the Fiesta Bowl, and the Huskers won the game and the national championship.

In 1996, the warts began to show in the system. No. 3 Florida won the national championship by upsetting top-ranked Florida State in the Sugar Bowl. The Pac-10 and the Big Ten didn't participate in the alliance, opting to send their champions to the much more lucrative Rose Bowl. In 1996, No. 2 Arizona State was upset by No. 4 Ohio State in the Rose Bowl—avoiding what could have been a split championship between the Gators and Sun Devils. The next season, a split occurred, as No. 1 Michigan topped Washington State in the Rose Bowl while No. 2 Nebraska defeated No. 3 Tennessee in the Orange Bowl. Michigan was the top team in the Associated Press poll; sentimental favorite Nebraska, in coach Tom Osborne's final season, topped the coaches' poll.

After the split national championship in 1997, SEC commissioner Roy Kramer helped develop the Bowl Championship Series. All six major conferences committed their champions to the format, with the Rose Bowl opening its doors to teams outside the Big Ten and the Pac-10 for the first time. The BCS also included two at-large teams, which were determined by a formula based on the writers' and coaches' polls, several computer rankings, strength of schedule, and overall record.

For the next five years, amid griping about some rankings here and there, a consensus national champion was crowned. The system, it would seem, worked. And then came 2003, and the fecal matter hit the oscillator. USC, the top team in the nation, was ranked third in the BCS standings and kept out of a title game. Oklahoma finished first in the final BCS standings, even though it lost in the Big 12 championship game. LSU took second in the standings and went on to beat the Sooners in the Sugar Bowl. USC, meanwhile, beat Michigan in the Rose Bowl. The Trojans took first in the AP poll; LSU was first in the coaches' poll, and we had yet another split championship.

The BCS came under fire again in 2004, when undefeated Auburn was left out of the title picture, and the nation's two other undefeated teams (USC and Oklahoma) played for the national title. In the end, a true national champion (USC) was again crowned, but the AP viewed the system as being so bastardized that it demanded its poll be pulled from the BCS rankings . . . presumably so that writers could go back to bitching about a process that they refuse to take part in. Beginning in the 2006 season, a new game will determine a national champion—separate from the four BCS bowls. Two more teams will be entered into the BCS standings, but it's still the top two teams in the BCS rankings that compete for the title.

Meanwhile, screams from the media were targeted at the coaches, whose votes—unlike those from journalists—were private. The pressure worked: in May 2005, the American Football Coaches Association ruled that coaches' final regular season ballots would become public.

The decision, naturally, was an idiotic one. You know who else doesn't have to reveal the way they voted? Members of the Academy of Motion Picture Arts and Sciences. Why? Because their votes are based on either predisposed bias, entrenched political loyalty, or, in the case of best short-form documentary, pick-the-funniest-name haphazardness. (And more likely than not, some of them allow their assistants and publicists to vote in their stead—just like the coaches.) Yet, for some reason, movie fans aren't asking for a six-film playoff series to determine Best Picture.

The Oscars are subjective. So is the NCAA, in both football and basketball. For all of the finality that the NCAA men's basketball tournament offers, nearly half of its teams are subjectively selected, and all of its teams are subjectively seeded.

In football, the entire process is subjective. Deal with it. Want a "plus one" format? Explain to the No. 1 team in the nation why it has to play two extra games just to stay No. 1. And then explain to the No. 5 team in the nation why it's on the outside looking in on the "top" four teams. Same thing goes for the No. 9 team in an 8-team format, the 17th team in a 16-team format, and the 25th team in a 24-team format. There's always going to be some team whose fans are going to feel they wuz robbed. (While you're at it, explain to the Rose Bowl how it'll make a fraction of the money it makes now as a quarterfinal in a playoff series.)

Like I said, the BCS isn't perfect. No system is going to be unless you eliminate the conference format and make every single Division I team independent and free to craft the toughest schedules they can—because strength of schedule is the crux of most BCS debates. It's something, on an annual basis, that teams just can't control. They are at the mercy of their conferences. And you know what? That's sports.

The BCS remains one of the worst ideas in the history of sports because, quite frankly, it tries to be everything to everyone. Judging by the last 30 years of NCAA football, there won't be a split championship every season. When there is one, perhaps fans should just deal with it rather than turning the season into an unending debate between warring factions of Bubbas, arguing about computer rankings when the majority of them refer to a computer in casual conversations as "the TV what has the words in it."

Perhaps it's time to stop spending so much time overanalyzing something that, at most, affects four or five teams every season. Most important, perhaps it's time for college football fans to realize that the folks in the sports media that advocate a tournament-style playoff format work for corporations that have quite a financial interest in seeing such a format implemented—competitive fairness and common sense be damned.

THE TOP 25 WORST IDEAS IN SPORTS HISTORY

PART 13

Turning the MVP into the Best Player Award

When the Numbers Just Don't Add Up

HAVE YOU ever been to a sporting event in which the crowd began a spontaneous chant of *M-V-P*? There's usually no hyperbole involved; thousands of people, in unison, proclaiming that one individual player has that much impact on the success of the team.

If only fans were the ones who decided such accolades. Increasingly, the Most Valuable Player awards in each major team sport have become symbolic citations for the most dominating player—statistically—in the league rather than the player who had the greatest influence on his team. It all comes down to a divergence in values. Sportswriters and players only see empirical value; fans see value in more spiritual terms.

Two easy litmus tests can determine a true MVP candidate. The first test is to measure how much and in how many different ways a player helped his team. That means looking beyond the flashiest statistics to quantify situational and defensive impact, throwing in the subjective measurement of his effectiveness as a leader. That's why Andre Dawson's MVP in 1987 with the Chicago Cubs was a joke; voters couldn't look past his 49 home runs—on a team 18.5 games out of first place—to see Will Clark's unbelievable season in which he led the NL West champion San Francisco Giants in every offensive category not named "stolen bases."

With that first test, Alex Rodriguez would have deserved his 2003 MVP award for his incredible season (47 home runs, 118 RBIs, 124 runs) with the Texas Rangers. Add those stats with a .989 fielding percentage at shortstop, and A-Rod appeared to be the total package. Yet the Rangers were 71–91, last place in the AL West, and 25 games out of first. That's where the second test comes in: where would Team X be without Player Y in the lineup?

Take A-Rod out of the Texas lineup, and the team still had big bats in Rafael Palmeiro, Juan Gonzalez, and Hank Blalock. Rodriguez made a bad team into an offensive powerhouse; without him, the Rangers were still going to be about as bad as they were with him. Meanwhile, if you took Carlos Beltran—and his 102 runs, 26 home runs, 100 RBIs, and 41 stolen bases—off the 2003 Kansas City Royals, that team isn't anywhere near 83–79 and seven games out of first place . . . unless you have a lot more faith in Angel Berroa and Raul Ibanez than I do.

The same test could be successfully applied to dozens of "best player award" decisions, such as Magic Johnson's 1990 NBA MVP on a Lakers team that also featured James Worthy, Byron Scott, and A. C. Green in the starting lineup. Meanwhile, the Philadelphia 76ers were Atlantic Division champions for one reason: Charles Barkley, who averaged 25.2 points and 11.5 rebound per game . . . playing next to Mike Gminski. Sir Charles received more first-place MVP votes (38) than Magic (27) but lost the award to the Lakers point guard on total points.

While our stats-obsessed society would appear to easily absorb most of the blame for this transformation from "most valuable" to "numerically superior" player awards, statistics that could have identified a player's value have been systematically eliminated or ignored. Major League Baseball dumped the game-winning RBI stat about eight years after it was implemented, in 1980. Writers complained that it was an empty stat; proponents vowed it accurately identified clutch hitters. In the NHL, game-winning goals are rarely considered when voting on the Hart Trophy winner occurs. (The Conn Smythe, for playoff MVP, remains an award dedicated to the player most valuable to his team's playoff run.)

The "best player award" mind-set can be better attributed to our cult of celebrity. To us, it makes sense to give the MVP to the biggest offensive star on the best team, such as Wayne Gretzky, who won nine Harts in the 1980s. But in reality, having the best numbers doesn't always equal having the greatest impact on a team's success.

The XFL

Misunderstood Genius . . .
but Also an Unmitigated Disaster

TO: Loyal reader.

FROM: Me.

RE: That chapter entitled "The Premature Death of the XFL."

MEMO: Aw, who the hell am I kidding? The XFL was an absolute abomination.

It was too ambitious. Vince McMahon is a master showman, but there's a thin line between hyperbole and idiocy; and it was sheer lunacy to vow to revolutionize pro football and take down the NFL—especially with talent that could be called Division I mid-major at best and scab worthy at worst. You can't convince a football fan that what they're watching is good football if in fact it's horrendously bad football. Check out the attendance figures for the Arizona Cardinals for the last decade and see what I mean.

The marketing of the XFL undermined whatever momentum the league might have been able to regain after its inauspicious debut. Wrestling fans quickly decided that the finished product didn't deliver on the scandalous promises of its hype, which guaranteed cheerleaders dating players and other such frivolity. Football fans tuned in to those early weeks to see a revolution;

instead, they saw games that had the drama and quality of NFL exhibition contests. The hype inflated the expectations of both these key constituencies; the XFL's first fledgling weeks permanently punctured them.

I still believe that the product improved to the point where the XFL should have been given a second chance by fans and a second season by the networks. But I can't ignore the facts: losses of close to $70 million between NBC and the WWF; ratings that make NHL games on cable TV look like the finale of *M*A*S*H*; and a legacy of failure that puts the XFL in the same league as blondes, lawyers, and Michael Jackson when it comes to sure-thing punchlines.

Even noted comedian Bill Belichick got in on the act. In 2004, after *Monday Night Football* was ripped for a towel-dropping skit involving Terrell Owens and Nicollette Sheridan, the New England Patriots coach was quoted by the *Boston Herald* as saying, "If preserving the integrity of the game and presenting it in the right way involves getting lower ratings, then that's what we're going to have to accept. If that's what we have to do, if that's the deal, then that's the deal. This can't become the XFL."

Alas, XFL, we hardly knew ye; but when we did, it wasn't pretty.

Whatizit!

Whatwasit? Crap

*O*N OCCASION *in this book, it becomes imperative to share an extraordinary point of view on a given theme. The only way to truly accomplish that is through the appointment of a guest essayist on said topic. This is one such instance.*

Hi . . . meesa called Jar-Jar Binks! Yousa may remember meesa from such films as *Star Wars* episodes one, two, and threesa!

Mine don't have to tell yousa that mine knows a bad mascot when mine sees one. When da *Phantom Menace* came out in da year of 1999, mine was 'sposed to be da new Ewok. Jar-Jar lunch boxes. Jar-Jar Underoos. Jar-Jar talking dolls. (*Meesa need a hug!*)

Okeyday, so mine wasn't so popular. Everyone basically hated meesa. So much that mine was in *Attack of the Clonesas* for only about 30 seconds.

But *ex-squeeeeeeeze* me! Compared to Whatizit, mine is more popular than Yoda and Han Solo put together!

Whatizit is da mascot of da Summer Olympics in da city of Atlanta in 1996. Historically, Olympic mascots were animals, like tigers, wolves, and bears. Den came Whatizit! Like meesa, heesa was a computer-generated creature. But while meesa looked like the love child of Big Bird and a horned toad, Whatizit could transform into anything, like a soccer ball or a base-a-ball.

An adorable plush version of Whatizit, the cuddly and deeply disturbing mascot of the 1996 Atlanta Summer Olympics.

Uh-oh! Da problem with Whatizit—besides dat dumb-assa name—was that when heesa wasn't a soccer ball or a base-a-ball, heesa looka like a sperm cell—a walking, talking sperm cell . . . with a constant smile of uncomfortable satisfaction on his face!

Ex-squeeeeeeze me?

The media no like-ah Whatizit. The fans no like-ah Whatizit. One website called him "post-Chernoble navel lint." Heesa became a bigger laughingstock than meesa ever was!

Before da Summer Olympics, da Atlanta organizers decided to change da name of their animated mascot to Izzy, so da children would like it better. And what father wouldn't want his daughter to cuddle in bed every night clutching a stuffed sperm cell?

Not meesa!

White Broadcasters on Black Athletes

All the Racial Sensitivity of a Lynch Mob

THERE'S NO doubt that off-the-cuff remarks and politically incorrect humor have their place in sports. Without them, what the hell would we talk about on the golf course for three hours?

But their place really isn't on football pregame shows. Or on basketball radio broadcasts. Or coming from Civil War scholars like Jimmy the "Greek" Snyder. Here's a happy little waltz down memory lane, aka the Great White Way.

Howard Cosell, *Monday Night Football*, 1983

While covering a Washington Redskins game for ABC, the late great Cosell watched receiver Alvin Garrett—who happened to be black—catch a pass. What Cosell said next has been reported as both "That little monkey gets loose, doesn't he?" as well as the more-to-the-point "Look at that little monkey run!" The network's phone lines lit up with complaints, but ABC stood by its controversial commentator. Cosell later copped to racial insensitivity in his comment but did not apologize for it. A similar incident occurred 13 years later, when CBS basketball commentator Billy Packer called Georgetown

University star Allen Iverson a "tough monkey." Packer apologized and went unpunished.

Jimmy the "Greek" Snyder, 1988

Snyder had one of the most respectable jobs on network television during the 1980s: advocating illegal sports gambling by picking games against the point spread on CBS's football pregame show. But little did we know he was also moonlighting as a professor of anthropology! On Martin Luther King's birthday, a television reporter in a Washington, D.C., restaurant asked Snyder about the progress that black athletes had made in professional sports. Professor the Greek pontificated, according to *Time* magazine, that "the black is a better athlete to begin with because he's been bred to be that way . . . because of his high thighs and big thighs that goes up into his back. This goes back all the way to the Civil War, when . . . the slave owner would breed his big black to his big woman so that he could have a big black kid." He went on to say that there wasn't much left for the white athlete in sports, especially if the blacks start taking over coaching jobs.

CBS ended its 12-year relationship with Snyder shortly after his comments made national news.

David Halberstam, Miami Heat Radio Play-by-Play, 1997

Halberstam (no, not the Pulitzer Prize–winning journalist . . . the other David Halberstam) was broadcasting a Heat game against Golden State when Miami's John Crotty, who is white, made an impressive play. "Thomas Jefferson would have been proud of that pass from Crotty," Halberstam said, according to *Jet* magazine. (Crotty, you see, was a graduate of the University of Virginia, founded by Jefferson.) Halberstam then added a second thought: "When Thomas Jefferson was around, basketball was not invented yet, but those slaves working at Thomas Jefferson's farm, I'm sure they would have made good basketball players."

Several Heat players were outraged; Halberstam was fined $2,500 by the NBA; and Miami cut ties with him in 1998.

Rush Limbaugh, *ESPN NFL Sunday Countdown*, 2003

ESPN hired the radio talk show host to serve as the "voice of the fan" on its football pregame show. Limbaugh would give commentaries on players, teams, and trends in the NFL and occasionally debate the ex-jocks on the show about the league that he never came close to playing in. In September 2003, Limbaugh shared his opinion on Philadelphia Eagles quarterback Donovan McNabb—specifically, that McNabb was being overrated by the media because it wants to see a black quarterback succeed in the NFL: "I think what we've had here is a little social concern in the NFL. The media has been very desirous that a black quarterback do well. There is a little hope invested in McNabb, and he got a lot of credit for the performance of this team that he didn't deserve. The defense carried this team." This vast media conspiracy was no doubt news to players such as Andre Ware, Rodney Peete, Tony Banks, Charlie Batch, Kordell Stewart, Akili Smith, and Quincy Carter, who never seemed to warrant the affirmative-action activism that McNabb received.

Limbaugh, not exactly universally beloved to begin with, was lambasted for the remark and further condemned for not backing away from his comments later in the week on his radio program. "All this has become the tempest that it is because I must have been right about something," he said.

ESPN threw Limbaugh under the bus, declining to offer its support. He resigned from the pregame show three days after his comments on McNabb, saying in a statement, "My comments this past Sunday were directed at the media and were not racially motivated. I offered an opinion. This opinion has caused discomfort to the crew, which I regret. I love *NFL Sunday Countdown* and do not want to be a distraction to the great work done by all who work on it."

Fans were only left to wonder how comments about the media's coddling a player because he is black could have nothing to do with race . . .

Maz Is Elected to Cooperstown
The Bar Is Lowered to Limbo Levels

REMEMBER the Soup Nazi on *Seinfeld*?

I'm the Cooperstown Nazi. If you're not one of the truly legendary players in the history of Major League Baseball . . . *No plaque for you!* If I can't mention you in the same breath as Cobb, Young, Ruth, Mantle, Mays, and Aaron without choking back the bile of mediocrity . . . *No plaque for you!*

My Hall of Fame is for mythical heroes. My Hall of Fame demands that a player be one of the top five or six of his generation or have the kind of timeless impact on the game where his contributions are acknowledged long after he stopped lacing up the cleats. If I ran the National Baseball Hall of Fame, I'd purge the rolls of about 75 percent of the current honorees. There are just too many all-stars, award hogs, and stat whores masquerading as baseball royalty for my tastes.

My criteria are, admittedly, rigid. I don't simply rely on the usual litany of statistical benchmarks that signal automatic induction. Most of them are miserable measurements of talent and achievement anyway. (It was painful, for example, to see the once great Dale Murphy hit a combined .152 in the

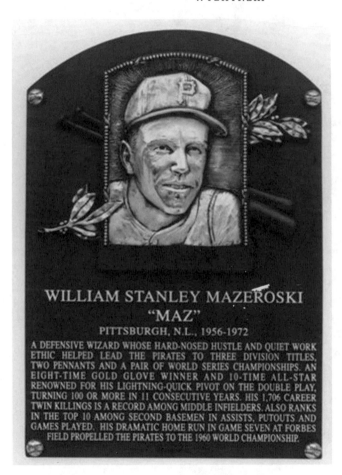

WILLIAM STANLEY MAZEROSKI
"MAZ"
PITTSBURGH, N.L., 1956-1972
A DEFENSIVE WIZARD WHOSE HARD-NOSED HUSTLE AND QUIET WORK
ETHIC HELPED LEAD THE PIRATES TO THREE DIVISION TITLES,
TWO PENNANTS AND A PAIR OF WORLD SERIES CHAMPIONSHIPS. AN
EIGHT-TIME GOLD GLOVE WINNER AND 10-TIME ALL-STAR
RENOWNED FOR HIS LIGHTNING-QUICK PIVOT ON THE DOUBLE PLAY,
TURNING 100 OR MORE IN 11 CONSECUTIVE YEARS. HIS 1,706 CAREER
TWIN KILLINGS IS A RECORD AMONG MIDDLE INFIELDERS. ALSO RANKS
IN THE TOP 10 AMONG SECOND BASEMEN IN ASSISTS, PUTOUTS AND
GAMES PLAYED. HIS DRAMATIC HOME RUN IN GAME SEVEN AT FORBES
FIELD PROPELLED THE PIRATES TO THE 1960 WORLD CHAMPIONSHIP.

Bill Mazeroski's Baseball Hall of Fame plaque. (Courtesy of National Baseball Hall of Fame Library, Cooperstown, NY) final two years of his career while chasing 400 home runs—knowing what that magic number meant for his Hall of Fame chances—and settling on 398.)

I'm not looking for stats; I'm yearning for something imperceptible. Whatever it was, Ruth had it. Mays had it. Nolan Ryan had it. Roger Clemens had it. Cal Ripken Jr. had it. Don Sutton, however, didn't.

Neither did Bill Mazeroski, who was elected to the National Baseball Hall of Fame in 2001 by the Veterans Committee. He was passed over by the writers for 15 years before finally leaving the ballot. The veterans usually reserved their votes for ex–big leaguers who made their marks as managers or for special cases such as former Negro League players. But occasionally, they take it upon themselves to champion a player whose skill sets and contributions to the game may have been overlooked by the baseball writers upon his initial candidacy. Such was the case with Mazeroski.

Maz played from 1956 to 1972 with the Pittsburgh Pirates. As far as I can tell, he's represented in that big room in upstate New York with the likes of Babe Ruth and Cy Young for the following:

1. Hitting the World Series–winning home run in Game 7 against the New York Yankees in 1960
2. Being one of the best—if not the best—defensive second basemen in the history of the game, turning more double plays than anyone else at that position

And that's it. Maz has a .260 lifetime batting average, a .299 on-base percentage, fewer than 2,100 hits, fewer than 150 home runs, fewer than 1,000 RBIs. If he's in the Hall of Fame because of his glove, I've got two words for you: Mickey Vernon. The former Washington Senator holds the National

League record for double plays turned by a first baseman. He also led the league in batting average twice and had more hits (2,495), RBIs (1,311), home runs (172), and runs (1,196), as well as a higher on-base percentage (.359) and batting average (.286), than Mazeroski did.

Statistically, Vernon was the better player. Perhaps Maz is in the Hall of Fame based on one memorable postseason home run? If so, Kirk Gibson is somewhere, weeping.

Bill Mazeroski was a great player and an even better person. His tear-filled speech at his induction was genuinely moving. But all of that and a token will get you on the Garden State Parkway—it should have no bearing on achieving baseball immortality.

The Night the Lights Went on at Wrigley

Sung to the Tune of "The Night the Lights Went Out in Georgia," by Vicki "Mama's Family" Lawrence

In nineteen sixteen
The Chicago Cubs
Moved their bats and their batting gloves
To a ball field that by twenty-seven
Was officially Wrigley;
Ivy on the walls
And bleacher tans
Babe's called shot, score-board by hand
Gallons of beer to make your stomach
All kinds of jiggley;
There was no talk of lights
Until forty-one
But that night-game plan was aban–doned

After Pearl Harbor, Uncle Sam
Got all the equipment;
In nineteen eighty-eight
The owners made demands
Tribune wanted lights on top of the stands
The neighborhood complained but the neighborhood
Couldn't resist it;
(Chorus)
That's the night when the lights went on at Wrigley
That's the night they pissed off traditional fans
Fans think the Cubs should just play in the sun–light
They like night games as much as they like Steve Bart–man;
On the night of eight
Eight eighty-eight
Wrigley day baseball was to meet its fate
But Jesus made the rain end the game
In the fourth inning;
But the very next night
With the Mets in town
The night was clear, and the fans did frown
Maybe Jesus was really a Cards fan
From the beginning;
In his grave
Mr. Wrigley did twitch
When the Tribune Company flipped that switch
And 40,000 Cubbie fans were
All illuminated;

Purists bitched and
Moaned and cried
And a little piece of Chicago died
The fans could see clearly
And clearly were inebriated;
(Chorus)
That's the night when the lights went on at Wrigley
That's the night when the magic started to die
By twenty-oh-five it was up to 30 night games
Somewhere up there, Harry Carey's starting to cry . . .

Michael Jordan's Career Choices

In Baseball and D.C., No One Wanted to Be like Mike

FROM 1986 to 1993, Michael Jordan came about as close to ascending to some sort of athletic deity as a 6-feet-6-inch kid from North Carolina could. It's only fitting that his nickname was "Air" because Michael was all around us. He was the shoes on your feet, the jersey on your back, and the reason that you bought that too-tight pair of underwear. He was the poster on your wall, the cartridge in your Nintendo, and the reason that you were eating that Big Mac. At one point, His Airness became effluvium: Michael Jordan cologne, anyone? He was even in a Bugs Bunny cartoon, joining such rarified company as Porky Pig, Edward G. Robinson, and Adolf Hitler.

He averaged 33.4 points per game from 1986 to 1993, won three Most Valuable Player awards, and won three consecutive NBA championships with the Chicago Bulls. Jordan epitomized the difference between the perception of perfection and actually being made of Teflon—if Jordan had any chinks in his armor, such as gripes from teammates about his attitude and his occasionally selfish play, they couldn't stick.

But in 1993, there was the double whammy: the murder of his father, James, in South Carolina and a slew of allegations about his outrageous gambling debts on golf games and in casinos. Jordan soured on the spotlight and stunned the world when he retired from the NBA to attempt a career as a Major League Baseball player.

He signed a minor league contract with the Chicago White Sox and tried to make the majors in spring training of the 1994 season. Problem was that Jordan, despite great speed, was a below-average hitter and an atrocious outfielder—ironic, considering that he was one of the most effective defenders in the history of basketball.

To the White Sox's credit, they opted not to make Jordan a traveling sideshow—like that goat-with-one-horn "unicorn" I saw at the circus one year—and sent him down to the AA Birmingham Barons. He went on to hit an anemic .202, with three home runs in 127 games, and led the Southern League with 11 errors in the outfield.

Even though some of his numbers were better than expected (55 RBIs, 30 stolen bases) and he drew enormous crowds wherever the Barons traveled, Jordan did what no one had seen him do before: flounder at something to which he had dedicated himself. He quit baseball after that season for rumored reasons ranging from the baseball players' strike to the White Sox's potentially leaving him in AA for a second season. On March 18, 1995, Jordan announced his return to the Chicago Bulls. He would lead the Bulls to a second threepeat (1996–1998), lead the league in scoring three times, and secure three consecutive NBA Finals MVP awards. He retired on top in January 1999, saying he was "99.9 percent sure" that he would remain off the court . . . and then wouldn't you know it, he came back again, joining the Washington Wizards a year and a half after becoming a part owner and president of basketball operations with the team. It's always that 0.1 percent you can never count on . . .

Jordan's second return stint in the NBA mirrored his disastrous baseball career. He was the biggest draw in the history of the franchise, the catalyst for a string of sellouts whose financial reverberations helped turn the area around D.C.'s MCI Center arena into one of the city's best shopping and dining destinations. At the same time, he was a shell of his former self, as his scoring average dipped to its lowest level since his second year in the league and the Wizards failed to make the postseason in both of his seasons in Washington. Jordan used to make the players around him better—he won three titles with Randy Brown and Jud Buechler, for Pete's sake—but didn't come close to elevating his team into a contender.

He retired for a third time in April 2003, claiming that he wanted to focus on working behind the scenes to make Washington a playoff team. The next month, the Wizards cut him loose as an executive, citing a string of bad coaching hires (Gar Heard, Leonard Hamilton) and player signings (Charles Oakley, Jerry Stackhouse). It was the first time that Jordan had been dropped from a basketball team since he was a sophomore in high school, and he wasn't happy: "I am shocked by this decision and by the callous refusal to offer me any justification for it," he said in a statement after meeting with the Wizards. Boy . . . someone in Washington obviously wasn't aware of the Jordan Rules.

In baseball, Jordan looked inept. In his second basketball comeback, Jordan looked antiquated. The guy convinced a generation of basketball fans that a man could fly and then showed them how hard he could fall.

Overexpansion in the 1990s

A Case of Too Much, Too Soon, and Too Bad

BEFORE I became an infallible sports historian/award-winning journalist, I used to work in market research for a certain fast-food burger chain that sounds like "Dick Monalds." My job was to find out where people were coming from to buy their food at said restaurant and whether other locations were necessary to fully blanket a certain geographic area. It was a challenging job to say the least: Some trucker dude once propositioned me in the men's room. Another time, a homeless woman told me that her entire family was waiting across the street to kill me. And, of course, how can I forget the gas leak that threatened to blow up the entire burger joint . . . chicken nuggets and all.

In the end, I felt as though I was helping a popular and established business to increase its market share. That was until the day that I drove past one of the restaurants that I had worked in and saw that it had closed down for good. Yet down the street to the left was a new "Dick Monalds" and about seven blocks beyond it was another new "Dick Monalds." New franchises had watered down the customer base until the oldest store couldn't keep up with the new kids on the block and was forced to close.

But that's what overexpansion does, especially in professional sports: it thins the product's talent level, whether it's a bullpen in baseball or a fourth line in hockey. Sometimes, it places franchises in regions that simply don't have a need for a particular sport and then must siphon money away from the league via revenue sharing just to stay afloat. The 1990s were a boom time for unfortunate expansion in pro sports. Consider the following.

National Hockey League

In 1991, the NHL had 21 teams; by 2004, it had 30. The reason for the expansion explosion was twofold: first was a desire by the league's owners to tear into expansion start-up fees like a lion attacking a gazelle on the Serengeti; second was the ill-conceived thought by former NBA lackey turned NHL commissioner Gary Bettman that spreading hockey to diverse American locales would create a populist boom for the league and huge television revenues. (As of 2005, the plan worked so well that the NHL was forced into a broadcast deal with NBC that even public access television producers could snicker at.)

The decade began well, with the San Jose Sharks. But then came the Ottawa Senators in 1992, seen at the time as merely a concession to Canadian fans who were worried that the majority of their teams would migrate to the United States. (And in the next few seasons, both the Winnipeg Jets and Quebec Nordiques did just that.) The Senators were perennial league door-mats until 1996, when they made the playoffs for the first time. Although they were a traditional postseason team by 2005, the Sens remain a franchise that generates more apathy than excitement for the majority of NHL fans.

The Mighty Ducks of Anaheim entered the league in 1993 and proceeded to see their attendance erode over the next decade. By 2005, they were for sale, and the league was considering a takeover. The Florida Panthers arrived with the Ducks, and while they've been able to draw fans, the Panthers have been one of the league's financially shakiest clubs. Florida claimed to have lost at least $17 million during the NHL's cancelled 2004–2005 season—but that reduced their annual losses by 60 percent. (Ironically, both the Ducks and the Panthers made the Stanley Cup Finals within their first decade of operation.) In 1998, Nashville entered the NHL. By 2004, rumors of the Predators' relocation or contraction made more headlines than the team did. Only a sweetheart arena deal was keeping the Preds afloat. In 1999, the Atlanta Thrashers came into the NHL, 19 years after the Flames left for Canada—because, evidently, it's a shrewd idea to give a city that has never consistently supported the Braves, Hawks, or Falcons a second chance at professional hockey.

Major League Baseball

The Tampa Bay Devil Rays (1998): Crappy name. Crappy stadium. Crappy records. And in 2004, six years after it entered the American League, it was outdrawn by a hockey team in the same city (Rays: 16,139 per game; Lightning: 17,820). You have to really, really try hard to get outdrawn by an NHL team if you're playing in a stadium with a capacity of close to 44,000.

National Basketball Association

The 1980s were an era of frequent and successful expansion for the NBA, as teams in Miami (1988), Orlando (1989), Minnesota (1989), and Charlotte

(1988) were born. (Charlotte later moved to New Orleans but was a standard of expansion success in its first several seasons in North Carolina.)

In the 1990s, a funny thing happened to commissioner David Stern: he forgot that the *N* in NBA didn't stand for *Nordic*. The Toronto Raptors and Vancouver Grizzlies entered the league in 1995, becoming the first franchises to offer exciting NBA action punctuated by the delicious smell of sizzling back bacon and caribou steaks. Toronto endured through a bad first "arena" (the Raptors played three-and-a-half seasons in SkyDome), some significantly injurious seasons, and little postseason success to maintain a fan base that averaged 19,095 spectators per home game from 2000 to 2004. Vancouver? Eh, not so good, hoser. The franchise—originally nicknamed the Mounties before the Royal Canadian Mounted Police and the dastardly Snidely Whiplash protested—saw its attendance drop in each of its five nonlockout seasons. Oh, and about that lockout: the abbreviated 1998–1999 season saw the Grizzlies average 16,719 per game, which was the highest total since its inaugural season. The following year, Canadian fans showed just how much they appreciated the lockout by dropping that average to 13,899.

The biggest embarrassment in franchise history came when Vancouver drafted guard Steve Francis out of Maryland in the 1999 NBA entry draft. At first, Francis refused to play for the Grizzlies because the team was too far away from his family in Maryland, because of the exchange rate, and because endorsement money wouldn't be there for someone playing in oblivion. Later, he told reporters that God didn't want him to play in Vancouver . . . which made sense to Grizzlies fans, seeing as how Gretzky hailed from Brantford, Ontario. Vancouver relocated to Memphis in 2001.

Sideline Reporters
Nice Blazer . . . Now Please Shut Up

(Trumpet fanfare)

ANNOUNCER: Movietone News, in association with the Boric Acid Distribution Consolidation and Happy Dancing Bear caramel snack cakes, presents GREAT MOMENTS IN SIDELINE SPORTS JOURNALISM.

(An elderly white man in a white lab coat appears, sitting behind a cluttered desk.)

DOCTOR DICKERSON: Hello . . . I'm Dr. Dickerson of the Tafoya Institute for Advanced Sports Broadcasting Study. Friends . . . while watching a football contest on television, have you ever wondered how information about the status of an injured player, the condition of the artificial turf, or the whereabouts of the defensive coordinator's elderly parents in the stands travels from the field to the announcers' booth? It's through an intricate communications system we here at the institute call "sideline reporting." Since 1994, the first year the NFL allowed sideline reporters on the field, every broadcasting crew worth its salt employs a comely vixen or studious gentleman to gather information during the game that could otherwise be collected by any sports information intern in the building. Without these sideline reporters, perhaps we'd never know the starting running back's nickname in college was "T-Money." Or we'd never hear those insightful interviews with the winning coach before halftime that offer such pearls of wisdom as "We're going to make some adjustments, but keep doing what we're doing."

Allow us a few moments to enlighten you about their exploits, won't you? Thank you.

(Title card: Lisa Guerrero, "Monday Night Football")

ANNOUNCER: Dateline, September 2003. Fetching Lisa Guerrero was hired to replace the somewhat-less-fetching Melissa Stark as the top sideline news-hound for the NFL's most important weekly television broadcast. Her qualifications? She was a cheerleader for the Los Angeles Rams. And she played "Volunteer Bimbo" in *Batman Returns*. And she helped host a sports comedy show with thespian Tom Arnold.

Although she spent the entire season staring at her notes more than the camera, Guerrero's biggest gaffe came after the 2003 season opener between the New York football Jets and the Washington football Redskins, a team that had raided the Jets for several free agents in the off-season. One of those signings was explosive wide receiver Laveranues Coles. Guerrero approached Redskins quarterback Patrick Ramsey after his team's win over the Jets.

GUERRERO: I saw you talking to Laveranues Coles, your ex-teammate [before the game]. What did he say to you?

ANNOUNCER: Ramsey was dumbfounded, being that he and Coles had just played their first regular season game together.

GUERRERO: I saw you talking to your ex-teammates before. What did you have to say to them?

ANNOUNCER: The valiant signal caller finessed whatever reply he could, seeing as he had never played for the Jets in his two NFL seasons with the

Redskins. Obviously, Guerrero forgot that Coles and Ramsey were now team-mates, an easy mistake to make, seeing as Coles only caught five of Ramsey's passes for 106 yards in the game. Lisa Guerrero was fired by ABC the following spring.

(Title card: Suzy Kolber, "ESPN Sunday Night Football")

ANNOUNCER: Dateline, December 2003. In a classic case of right place/wrong gender, ESPN reporter Suzy Kolber was macked on by inebriated former Jets quarterback Joe Namath during a New York home game against New England. The Hall of Famer slowly answered Kolber's first question, slurring his words like a recovering stroke victim. But the plucky Kolber pressed on, asking the clearly intoxicated Namath what it meant to him that the Jets were struggling that season.

NAMATH: I want to kiss you. I could care less about the team struh-guh-ling. What we know is that we can improve. Chad missed . . . Chad Pennington, our quarterback, missed the first part of the season, and we struh-ggled. We're looking to next season. We're looking to . . . uh . . . make a noise now, and I want to kiss you.

ANNOUNCER: As the aptly named "Joe Willie" babbled on, Kolber thanked him for "a huge compliment" and kicked it back upstairs to the announcing crew. Commentator Joe Theismann said, "Joe's just a happy guy." Then, with the best one-liner since Rob Reiner's mother said, "I'll have what she's having," analyst Paul McGuire replied, "Oh boy, is he happy."

Namath, a former pantyhose model, later apologized to Kolber, admitted that he had been drinking for several hours before kickoff, and entered a rehab program in January 2004. Still, the ESPN exchange remains Namath's best pass since 1977.

(Title card: Jim Gray, NBC)

ANNOUNCER: Dateline, October 1999. The World Series, in beautiful Atlanta, Georgia. As an honored member of the All-Century Team, Charlie Hustle, aka Peter Edward Rose Sr., was making his first sanctioned appearance at a Major League Baseball event since being banned for life after evidence surfaced that he bet on the Cincinnati baseball Reds while managing them. Jim Gray, eager to prove that bad sideline reporting isn't confined to buxom beauties in tailored blazers, asked Rose to admit that he had bet on baseball. Rose refused to admit anything and called himself a "small part of a big deal tonight." Gray went on to ask Rose the same question not once, not twice, but four times, including this nonpartisan beauty:

GRAY: Pete, it's been 10 years since you've been allowed on the field. Obviously, the approach that you have taken has not worked. Why not, at this point, take a different approach?

ANNOUNCER: Gray was slammed by fans, players, and peers for his spotlight-snatching foray into "gotcha" journalism. While Rose's eventual admission to betting on baseball exonerated the content of Gray's queries, it did not excuse his heavy-handed, badly timed inquisition. But at least Rose never tried to kiss him.

(Trumpet fanfare)

This has been GREAT MOMENTS IN SIDELINE SPORTS JOURNALISM. For Movietone News, goodnight, have a pleasant tomorrow, and remember to purchase war bonds to support the boys across the pond.

The 1994 Baseball Strike
One Strike . . . and the Fans Were Out

A GIANT victory parade unfurls down Ste-Catherine in downtown Montreal as Larry Walker, Moises Alou, and Pedro Martinez are lauded with the kind of fanatic platitudes usually reserved for champions named Beliveau, Lafleur, and Roy. A seemingly unbreakable home run record is shattered by a 28-year-old third baseman from Bishop, California, named Matt Williams. Tony Gwynn goes from being the best hitter of his generation to ascending into that pantheon of legendary batsmen inhabited only by Cobb, Williams, and Rose.

It all could have happened. It all should have happened. But the 1994 strike by Major League Baseball's players union ensured that it would never happen.

For years leading up to the strike, owners had been clamoring for a salary cap. Players weren't buying Major League Baseball's tales of financial woe in regard to its small-market teams. The result of this stalemate was a 232-day work stoppage that began on August 12, 1994; wiped out that year's postseason; and changed Major League Baseball for better, for worse, and forever.

The detrimental ripples from the strike were staggering. Fans were feeling an odd combination of anger and apathy, saying out of one side of their mouths, "Who cares, screw 'em all," and out of the other bellowing, "These bastards actually canceled the World Series!"

The strike came to an end on March 31, 1995, when an injunction by a U.S. district court judge banned ownership from establishing new labor rules with a new agreement with the union. Players traveled to a truncated spring training under the old labor agreement, and it took nearly two years to sign a new deal that featured a luxury tax and increased revenue sharing between franchises.

The league and its players lost millions of dollars, and no measurement could accurately reflect the amount of trust that disappeared between the sides. On the field, the game might have lost Gwynn's having a .400 season (he was batting .394), Williams's breaking the Roger Maris record of 61 home runs (the Giants slugger was just off Maris's pace at 43 homers), and a Montreal Expos postseason run that may have resulted in that franchise's first World Series championship—and potentially saved the team from total collapse over the following seasons and a relocation to Washington, D.C., in 2004.

In 1994, average attendance was 31,612 per game; in 1995, it plummeted to 25,260. A decade later, it was still short over a thousand fans (30,599). The owners' defeat in the negotiation resulted in average salaries inflating from $1.18 million in 1994 to $2.49 million in 2004.

How did baseball escape total collapse? First, they juiced the ball. We can pretend that they didn't, that the dramatic rise in home run production had something to do with expansion or watered down pitching or hitter's ballparks. But after the Black Sox scandal in 1919, home runs increased from 630 in 1920 to 937 in 1921—a 48.7 percent increase. As the Great Depression swept across the nation at the end of the decade, home runs took another jump, from 1,349 in 1929 to 1,565 in 1930. In the 1980s, as the game was tarred by player drug scandals and attitude problems, home runs went from 2.27 per 100 at bats in 1984 to 3.01 per at bat in 1987. In 1993, there were 4,030 home runs hit. In 1996, the first full season after the strike, there were 4,962 home runs hit.

Now, the X factor in this home run derby is steroid use. It's another ripple from the strike: players juiced while ownership and Major League Baseball danced around the issue because, as offense increased, so did their revenues.

But it took more than artificial offense to save baseball after the strike. It took Cal Ripken's consecutive-games record. It took Mark McGwire and Sammy Sosa's duel to break Maris's record. And it took the rebirth of the New York Yankees' dynasty. All of these things dramatically increased interest in a sport that appeared headed for oblivion.

This entry was originally much higher on the list—much, much higher. But there's no denying that the desperate times that baseball faced in 1994 resulted in desperate measures that have improved the product significantly. "There were a lot of new ballparks. A change in the economic system was critical because it created much more competitive balance. The wild card and interleague play have worked," said commissioner Bud Selig in an interview with *USA Today*.

Selig referred to the post-strike years as a "golden era" for baseball. While no one should go that far—there are still grizzled old foamers who refuse to come back to the game—there's no question that some good did come out of this abominable idea.

Celebrity Nonsingers Tackling the National Anthem

Oh, Say Can You Suck?

BEFORE A sporting event, you might hear the "Star-Spangled Banner" being performed by a soloist from the local church, a songbird from the team's promotions department, or perhaps an up-and-coming country-music artist. As long as they can hit the high notes and remember 95 percent of the words, they're qualified to honor Americans with the singing of our national anthem. (In cases where "O Canada" is also performed, the word requirement drops to about 27 percent.)

Sometimes, teams and arenas opt for a little more star power in their pregame entertainment. Marvin Gaye crooned a sexy anthem at the 1983 NBA All-Star Game. Aretha Franklin sang an epic version of "America the Beautiful" at Wrestlemania III. And who can forget Whitney Houston's stunning and quite lengthy "Star-Spangled Banner" at Super Bowl XXV, smack dab in the middle of Gulf War I?

But most of the time, going the celebrity route is an unmitigated disaster. Like when the New Jersey Nets had Olympic gold medalist Carl Lewis sing the anthem on December 1, 1993. Oh, he did just fine . . . until that "rockets' red glare" part. That's the point in which Carl's voice morphed into that of a slowly suffocating llama. He struggled through the next few lines with the crowd muttering and jeering. He then had the gall to say, before the song's most difficult passage, "I'll make up for it now." Carl sang "o'er the laaaand" and then stopped and started again with "o'er the laaaaand, of . . ." before singing "the free" in a deep voice (well . . . deep for Carl Lewis) in order to avoid another high-pitched catastrophe. The crowd laughed and mockingly cheered him as the song limped to its finish. Nothing is more uncomfortable than seeing one of the fastest men in the world have nowhere to run.

Then there was Lucy "Xena, Warrior Princess" Lawless in 1997, singing the anthem at a Detroit Red Wings/Anaheim Mighty Ducks game. Her rather pedestrian effort was masked by the fact that she was dressed like a candy striper at a VFW hospital. But things got really interesting when Lawless decided to take off her Uncle Sam jacket and raise her left arm to punctuate the end of the song . . . which inadvertently raised her left breast out of the red teddy she was wearing. Talk about lawless . . . and who knew that Disney put on *that* kind of pregame entertainment?

But the undisputed queen of horrendous celebrity anthems is Roseanne Barr, whose July 1990 rendition of the "Star-Spangled Banner" remains one of the single-most embarrassing moments in baseball history. San Diego Padres co-owner and *Roseanne* co-producer Tom Werner asked Barr to sing the anthem on Working Women's Night at Jack Murphy Stadium. Roseanne decided to honor her sisters in arm with a screeching version of the anthem that grew more ear-piercingly loud and appalling as the 30,000 fans in attendance booed in unison. She ended the song by scratching her crotch and spitting on the field, later claiming that the players in the dugout encouraged her to do so: "A lot of [them] said, 'You ought to scratch yourself and spit, like all of us do.' I thought it would be really funny."

Right . . . just like we all thought that Roseanne's sitcom would end gracefully or that she wasn't crazier than a pre–shock therapy R. P. McMurphy. See how perceptions can turn out to be astoundingly incorrect?

Unfortunately, the curse of celebrity singers doesn't end with the national anthem. Just ask Cubs fans that had the misfortune of being at Wrigley Field the day Ozzy Osbourne sang "Take Me Out to the Ball Game" in 2003. Or, as Ozzy interpreted it,

> Let's go out to the ball game
> Let's go out to the yarn
> Take me a nu-nu-nu-nu bee anna noo
> I don't remember why I have the net
> Let's go out to do yahwey
> Nu-nu-nu-nu-nu-nu
> Bory beer
> Two
> Three strikes you're out
> At the old ball game.

Ozzy Osbourne: the only man who could have made Harry Carey sound like Professor Henry Higgins by comparison.

The One-Player Panacea
Going for Broke and Achieving It

IN 1781, English astronomer Dr. William Herschel discovered the planet Uranus. In 1989, the Herschel Walker trade made Minnesota general manager Mike Lynn look like an ass.

The Vikings were coming off a season in which they advanced to the NFC division playoffs, losing to San Francisco. But the team had a glaring weakness at running back, ranking 22nd in the NFL in yards per carry. The team's leading rusher was named Darrin Nelson, followed by some guy named Allen Rice and some other guy named Alfred Anderson. Lynn—and Minnesota fans—knew that with the team's strong defense, a solid rushing game could elevate the Vikings into the NFL's elite.

But Lynn didn't want solid; he wanted spectacular. So on October 12, 1989, the Vikings made the single biggest trade—by volume and perhaps impact—in the history of the NFL when they sent a package of players and picks to Dallas for former Heisman Trophy winner Herschel Walker.

How big was this trade? Minnesota dealt Dallas Nelson, linebacker Jesse Solomon, defensive back Isaac Holt, linebacker David Howard, and defensive end Alex Stewart, along with conditional first- and second-round draft picks in 1990 and 1991 and a first-round pick and conditional third-round pick in 1992.

A world-class genealogist couldn't trace the various paths that these players and picks took following the trade. By 1992, and the end of Dallas's run of Minnesota picks, the Cowboys had acquired running back Emmit Smith (the NFL's all-time leading rusher), safety Darren Woodson (the best defensive back in Cowboys history), cornerback Kevin Smith, defensive tackle Russell Maryland, and cornerback Clayton Holmes as a result of the trade. Those players helped form the foundation of the Cowboys' early-1990s dynasty of three Super Bowl titles in four seasons.

But Dallas wasn't the only team that benefited from the deal. Through various transactions after the Walker trade, Pittsburgh was able to draft tight end Eric Green; New England drafted offensive linemen Eugene Chung and Pat Harlow; and San Francisco selected defensive lineman Dennis Brown—all with Minnesota's picks.

As for the aforementioned Mr. Walker, he didn't get close to his star-making 1988 season with the Cowboys (1,514 yards rushing, 505 yards receiving, 7 touchdowns). Walker never cracked the 1,000-yard rushing mark in his two and a half seasons with Minnesota. The Vikings lost the only playoff game in which Walker played, in 1989, and failed to make the postseason in his final two years. Critics claimed that the team had no idea how to use Walker or how to build around him. The Vikings cut Walker after the 1991 season; the following year he had 1,070 yards rushing for the Philadelphia Eagles, who ended up winning an NFC Wild Card game that season. In 1996, Walker actually rejoined the Cowboys to back up the running back that the team drafted as a result of the original trade (Smith).

Like Walker, Eric Dickerson was considered one of the most dominant running backs in the NFL, having gained over 1,200 yards in each of his first four seasons with the Los Angeles Rams (1983–1986). But he was disgruntled with the Rams, and the team traded him to Indianapolis in a three-team deal with Buffalo on Halloween 1987. The Colts—who were coming off a 3–13 season before the trade—got 1,011 yards rushing in nine games from Dickerson, helping the team earn its first playoff berth in a decade. The following season, he went for 1,659 yards. But Dickerson's tenure with the Colts didn't produce a second trip to the postseason, and soon he was at odds with the coaches and vice versa.

The Rams were able to make the postseason in their two post-Dickerson years, running to the NFC title game on the legs of Greg Bell (1,137 yards) in 1989—one of two players, along with six draft picks, that came over in the trade. Buffalo, meanwhile, acquired holdout linebacker Cornelius Bennett from the Colts; he would go on to help anchor the defense for the Bills' four AFC championship teams.

Of course, football isn't the lone victim when it comes to the vandalistic effects of the one-player panacea. There's also hockey, with the Philadelphia Flyers and a prodigy named Eric Lindros.

Dubbed the "Next One" by hockey prognosticators, he refused to play for the Quebec Nordiques, who drafted him No. 1 overall in 1991. So the Nords put him on the market, and the market boiled down to two teams: the Flyers and the New York Rangers. Both were convinced at one point that they had a deal in place for Lindros; an arbitrator ruled that the Flyers made their deal first. So an unbelievable package of goalie Ron Hextall, winger Chris Simon, center Mike Ricci, blue-chip offensive prospect Peter Forsberg, defensemen Steve Duchesne and Kerry Hoffman, $15 million, the Flyers' first-round picks in 1993 and 1994, and the Liberty Bell (just kidding) was sent to Quebec for the rights to a player that had never stepped on the ice for an NHL team.

The Nordiques moved to Colorado in 1995 and won the Stanley Cup in 1996 and 2001. The foundation for both championship teams could be traced back to the Lindros trade; besides the players who were directly involved, Colorado ended up with goalie Patrick Roy, winger Claude Lemieux, defenseman Uwe Krupp, winger Alex Tanguay, winger Adam Deadmarsh, defenseman Rob Blake, and winger Shjon Podein, using different parts related to the Lindros deal. The Rangers, who lost out on Lindros in 1991, won their first cup in 54 years in 1994. New York built a champion using the same players whom it was willing to deal for Lindros in a variety of other trades.

The Flyers? Well, they got a Hart Trophy season out of Lindros in 1995 and made it to the Stanley Cup Finals in 1997. But Philly could never win the big prize with "Big E," and after an infamous wallop by New Jersey defenseman Scott Stevens in the 2000 Eastern Conference finals, Lindros began a steady descent into offensive normality and a series of debilitating head injuries. In 2001, he was traded . . . to the New York Rangers.

Tie Games
Tie Goes to the Bummer

TEAM MARKETING Report does something called the fan cost index every year, in which it examines how much a family of four spends to attend a professional sporting event. This index is based on the assumption that the family purchases four tickets of average cost, two programs (one for son, one for dad), parking, two souvenir hats (one for dad and one for the son that didn't get the program), two small beers (for mom), and four small soft drinks and four hot dogs (again, for mom). In 2004, it would have cost this family $425 to see the New England Patriots play a home game and $382 to see the Washington Redskins. The Detroit Red Wings and the Philadelphia Flyers each cost $318 for a night. For that kind of money, don't you think that a family deserves a satisfying outcome to the game it's attending?

For the 1996–1997 NHL season, tie games made up 13.5 percent of all games played. For 2002–2003, years after the league created four-on-four overtimes to help break ties, such games made up 12.8 percent. What sane customer was going to pay to watch a sport where there's no clear winner 13 percent of the time? It was worse in Major League Soccer, where in 2004 the league saw 46 ties—or 31 percent of its regular season matches. In the NFL, tie games are much more rare. Most seasons go by with nary a tie game, thanks to the natural point structure of the sport and the sudden-death aspect of the 15-minute overtime. But the mere presence of ties in professional football is inexcusable. Again, what sane customer would buy a season ticket to a sport in which one-eighth of a team's home games could potentially yield no discernable victor?

In all three sports, tie games are factored into the standings, which is completely maddening—especially in the NHL, such as in the 1996–1997 season, when the Montreal Canadiens and Ottawa Senators both made the postseason after being four games under .500 in the regular season, each with 15 ties.

Proponents of tie games are traditionalists who believe that ties are a naturally occurring part of sports, especially in international soccer, where team point standings decide World Cup champions.

But in America, the tie game exists for one reason only: television. The NFL has a contractually allotted amount of time on a Sunday afternoon to finish a game. Hockey, which really shouldn't ever do anything to tick off the networks, has taken steps to produce an artificial winner in overtime through inventions such as four-on-four play and the shootout. They can't compare with a playoff overtime for sheer excitement, but TV doesn't want four-period wars of attrition 30 times a season.

The bottom line is that sports are about winners and losers. The problem is that professional leagues will never give us a refund if we don't get to see one or the other.

Asterisks*
*That Thing to the Left of This Sentence

WE USE them to signal footnotes in an annotated essay or bullet points in a list. An equation multiplying x by $2x$ would be totally incoherent if not for the benefit of an asterisk in between.

They also have their playful side. Look! *v* An owl!

Asterisks are quite powerful, literally changing the meaning of something by their mere presence. Especially when it comes to words like *f**k, a**h*l*, pu**y,* and *c*nt.* You know, *fork, anthill, putty,* and *cent*?

When Roger Maris hit 61 home runs to break Babe Ruth's single-season record in 1961, he did so playing in 161 games. Ruth, however, needed just 151 games to hit 60 in 1927. When Maris and Yankees teammate Mickey Mantle were racing toward the home run record in 1961, Major League Baseball commissioner Ford Frick, a close friend of Ruth's, said that there should be some "distinctive mark" in the records if the Bambino's record was broken in more than 154 games—the maximum number of games in which Ruth could have appeared back in 1927.

You know that old line about lies being repeated enough until everyone accepts them as the truth? Such was the case with that legendary asterisk next to Maris's single-season home run record—there never was one, because there never was an "official" baseball record book to put it in. The asterisk nevertheless became synonymous with Maris's record, so much so that actor-director Billy Crystal incorporated it into his 2001 film about Maris and Mantle, *61**.

Today, baseball fans are wondering if the recent wave of admitted steroid abusers should have their accomplishments saddled with a big fat * . . . for example, anyone who hit 73 home runs in a single season, say, around 2001.

Artificial performance enhancement is, however, only one of a number of factors that separate the accomplishments of today's players from those of Maris, Mantle, and DiMaggio, not to mention Ruth and Cobb. Here are a few of these factors, in no particular order: fourteen more teams than in 1927, thousands of miles of added travel, dieticians, strength coaches, arthroscopic surgery, tendon replacement, free-agent option years, the split-fingered fastball, artificial turf, domed stadiums, sports talk radio, one-inning closers, five-man rotations, digital slow-motion video, advanced scouting, and a little piece of heaven called Percocet.

It's the same story in every sport: the records remain, but the conditions under which they are broken are in constant flux in relation to when they were first set. Can anyone honestly say, for example, what Johnny Unitas's stats would have been if he faced today's maddening defense blitz packages in the NFL? Or what Wilt Chamberlain's final point total would have been in the "hack a Shaq" era of NBA defense, since the Stilt shot only .511 from the line during his career?

Comparing modern athletic achievement with that of the past, and vice versa, is now an experiment in speculation rather than empirical analysis. So where does it stop? Are we destined to become an asterisked society? (Generation *, perhaps?)

There's only one record book where an asterisk is absolutely necessary: Hollywood's. I don't know about you, but I don't want my kids to grow up thinking *The Mummy Returns* ($202,019,785 domestic box office gross) was more popular in its day than *Gone with the Wind* ($198,676,459 . . . but $1,240,554,000 when adjusted for about six decades of inflation.)

As God as my witness, I'll never go ****** again!

The Olympics TripleCast
Three Channels . . . One for Each Subscriber

A T SOME point in their centuries-old history, the Olympics may have had something to do with actual athletic competition and achievement, rather than financial windfalls, political posturing, and a country's orchestrating an opening ceremony that most resembles an electric acid freakout at a Jefferson Airplane concert.

The 1992 Summer Olympics in Barcelona looked like a veritable ATM machine for all parties involved. About $1.145 billion in net income was expected to be generated from all facets of the Games, including sponsorship money, ticket sales, stupid overpriced "Cobi, the Olympic Sheepdog mascot" T-shirts, and, of course, television rights.

NBC, expecting the Barcelona Games to be the most watched in the history of the Olympics on American television, doled out $401 million for exclusive broadcasting. (To put that in perspective, the gross domestic product of Western Samoa in 1992 was $400 million.) Rumor was that the original price was significantly lower, but the International Olympic Committee requested some sort of compensation for having to put up with Ahmad Rashad for two full weeks . . .

When you lay out that kind of coin, you're going to do whatever you can to see a return on your investment. NBC and sports television guru Dick Ebersol came up with something rather extraordinary: pay-per-view Olympic coverage in the form of the Olympics TripleCast. The plan called for three different 24-hour-a-day cable networks that specialized in either women's, men's, or team sports. Events would be shown live from 5:00 AM to 5:00 PM, and then the coverage would repeat for the next 12-hour cycle.

Let's start with the most glaring flaw in this incredible broadcasting folly: anyone who purchased the Olympics TripleCast was not watching NBC's Olympics coverage on commercial television. So even if the pay-per-view idea had been gangbusters, it would have been at the expense of NBC's own ratings, which in turn would have cost the network ad revenue.

In 1992, an estimated 250,000 homes subscribed to the pay-per-view service, whereas NBC and broadcasting partner Cablevision had predicted upwards of 2.7 million homes. But the reason that the TripleCast failed so spectacularly was simply how much the damn thing cost. A viewer had to pay $29.95 for a single day of events; $95 for seven days; $125 for the full 15 days of the Barcelona Games; or a sum of $170 for all 15 days and some bonus Olympics promotional materials (like a spiffy jacket, for example). The cost of the TripleCast soon became a national joke for a cable culture that was used to dropping under $30 for pay-per-view boxing and wrestling events; and while Barcelona had both sports, it certainly didn't have Michael Buffer or Jimmy "Superfly" Snuka.

Plus, if anything of note actually happened during the Olympics, NBC would show it on tape delay anyway. There was no necessity to buy the TripleCast beyond one's obsession over virtually ignored niche sports—NBC was actually relying on badminton and trapshooting fans to drive its economic engine.

Adding to the TripleCast's bad mojo was a slew of press stories detailing how soft the sales were for the service. Jokes from late-night comedians in their monologues certainly didn't help either. Letterman made it a nightly punchline; Leno famously quipped, "If they can get one more person to sign up for the TripleCast, it will be a Quadruplecast."

The final TripleCast subscription totals were juiced by deep discounts on the package, including a special "weekend rate" of $29.95. How much NBC and Cablevision actually lost on their joint pay-per-view venture is a point of debate but seems almost besides the point—it's sort of like calculating the loss of the soup spoons that went down with the *Titanic*.

It wasn't all doom and gloom for the Olympics TripleCast. Subscribers generally enjoyed the coverage, which was long on events and short on the prepackaged over-dramatized crap that NBC was shoveling on viewers every 10 minutes. It also opened up some eyes as to the potential of pay-per-view sports, paving the way for season-long subscription-based football, baseball, and hockey packages.

That being said, the Olympics TripleCast still goes down as one of the most ill-conceived, poorly promoted, and all-around bad ideas in sports history.

10-Cent Beer Night

"No beer and no TV make Homer something something."

A BRIEF excerpt from my forthcoming book *What I Would Do to Get 10-Cent Beers at a Ball Game*:

- Corral a herd of rabid weasels
- Perform a *Fear Factor*–style stunt involving a large submersible glass tub, five hundred giant Madagascar hissing cockroaches, and a bucket of chum
- Read *Boy Wonder: My Life in Tights*, the poorly received 1995 memoir by Burt "Batman's Robin" Ward cover to cover and then translate it into Yiddish
- Play for the Devil Rays

In 1974, Cleveland Indians fans didn't have to attempt any of those feats in order to ingest some bargain suds. Attendance at Municipal Stadium had been as lowly as the Indians' fortunes; in 1973, the team drew its smallest number of fans since World War II. So the team decided to draw spectators with the intoxicating temptation of booze, offering 10-ounce cups of Stroh's

An unidentified guard helps Cleveland Indians Tom Hilgendorf after he was hit by a chair during the infamous Beer Night mêlée on June 4, 1974. (AP Photo/Cleveland Press, Paul Tepley)

for 10 cents apiece throughout the game on June 4, 1974. It was a ploy that had worked at other major league stadiums in recent years . . . but this night would produce an entirely different result.

One week before Beer Night—the first game of the Indians' three-game set against the visiting Texas Rangers—a mêlée broke out between the teams during a game in Arlington. After the Rangers' Lenny Randle slid hard into Cleveland second baseman Jack Brohamer early in the game, Indians pitcher Milt Wilcox threw behind Randle's head during his next at bat. Randle bunted the next pitch toward first base. When Wilcox went after the ball, he took a stiff forearm from Randle. A brawl started after Randle reached first base, and Indians players were showered with beer as they left the field. (Good thing Ron Artest wasn't in the Cleveland dugout that night.)

So Indians fans were entering their team's game against the Rangers with a Texas-sized chip on their shoulders. Many of the 25,134 fans that attended the game also decided not to forgo their pregame beverage consumption, even though beer inside the stadium could be had for a dime.

The first sound of trouble came as early as the first inning, when people in the press box claimed to have heard small explosions in the crowd. By the second inning, a full-figured woman ran on the field and flashed the crowd from the on-deck circle. A naked man slid into second base during the fourth inning—hopefully, not headfirst. Fans leaped onto the field and mooned the lower deck. "I remember getting spit on a lot and having a lot of hot dogs thrown at me," future Cleveland manager Mike Hargrove, then a Texas first baseman, recalled some years later to the Associated Press. "Somebody threw a gallon jug of Thunderbird wine at me."

In the ninth inning, what had been comparable to an outrageous frat party turned into a dangerous situation for the teams and the fans. Cleveland, down 5–3 entering the bottom of the ninth, rallied to tie the game and had the winning run on third base. But jubilant fans—who by this time had consumed somewhere in the neighborhood of 60,000 cups of brew—began running onto the field. One got into an altercation with Rangers outfielder Jeff Burroughs—who altercated right back—and a big kerfuffle began around the two. This reportedly led to Rangers manager Billy Martin grabbing a bat, turning to his team, and exclaiming, "Let's get 'em, boys!" (The bat was later found broken.)

Hall of Fame umpire Nestor Chylak, who was bloodied with a flying chair, called the game for the Rangers. Nine fans were arrested for their roles in the riot. But all of that chaos didn't impress Indians management, as Cleveland did not alter its plans for additional 10-cent beer nights. American League president Lee MacPhail had to step in to cancel them . . . while also banning beer sales at Municipal Stadium for some time.

Chylak summed up the scene to the *Lorain Journal*: "We went as far as we could go, but you can't pull back uncontrollable beasts. The last time I saw animals like that was in the zoo."

The Designated Hitter
Depriving the World of Hundreds of David Wells At Bats

BRIAN DOWNING'S actions tell you everything that you need to know about the designated-hitter rule. As a member of the Texas Rangers, Downing was playing the last of his 2,344 major league games in 1992. He had been listed as a designated hitter in 824 of those games, yet Downing made a special request to his manager for his last hurrah: to be listed in the lineup as a second baseman rather than a DH.

It was a sensible request for anyone who has appreciated the unique stratagem of baseball or a "complete" ballplayer—one who excels on the field as well as at the plate. The designated hitter diminishes both aspects of baseball, besides providing a litany of other unfortunate dilemmas that far outweigh its diversionary benefits.

The DH had first been considered in the 1920s, that post-scandal era in baseball in which offense and gate receipts trumped common sense and tradition. The rule was adopted by several minor leagues during the 1940s, but Major League Baseball resisted it as a viable option for juicing run production, until the late 1960s. It was during that time that the American League saw a drop in offense—Carl Yastrzemski's .301 average in 1968 remains the lowest ever for an AL batting champion—and, more important, a drop in attendance. Indeed, the National League batting champ had a higher average than the AL's for 12 straight years, a streak that ended in 1973, the first season of the DH.

In 1969, the Triple-A International League decided to experiment with the DH for a season. As a result, the league's batting average climbed 17 points. The experiment ended after its initial season, but the American League's appetite was whetted. Championed by maverick Oakland A's owner Charlie O. Finley, the "designated pinch hitter" rule was instituted on a three-year trial basis via an 8–4 vote by American League owners. The National League nearly followed suit, but cooler heads prevailed.

Offense improved almost immediately. Players whose inept fielding would have relegated them to a spot on the bench in the National League were allowed to make believe they were Babe Ruth in the American League without the burden of, you know, actually having to play baseball.

I know that a lot of this designated hitter "debate" stems from the fact that some people (like yours truly) grew up watching a National League team while others grew up watching an American League team. It's like being born into two different sects of the same religion—we have opposing rectitude that is engrained and therefore impervious to rational discourse. But allow me to try anyway:

- The designated-hitter rule does not allow for as much managerial strategy as DH-free baseball. It goes beyond decisions such as pinch-hitting and the double switch, although the prevalence of both enhances play in the National League. What about simply filling out that day's lineup card? If a National League team's bench goes 10 deep, the manager has to decide every single game which player doesn't play; in the American League, the manager just decides which player won't be in the field. Is that really better for baseball?

- Bad hitters are still allowed to be hitters. Perhaps the most ludicrous argument for the use of a designated hitter is that pitchers, by and large, have the batting skills of an 11-year-old softball player; thus, having some slugger bat for him is better for the game. To those who believe this to be true, I ask a rather elementary question: would you have a problem with a second designated hitter, perhaps for that light-hitting shortstop? Or perhaps a third designated hitter, to bat for those catchers who just can't seem to hit a curveball? Maybe one day we can have nine players to play the field and then another nine to bat for them. Is that really better for baseball?
- The designated hitter is a pathetic crutch for incomplete players. Edgar Martinez is one of the best hitters in the history of baseball. But he only played 591 games in the field, compared with 1,412 as a designated hitter. If you don't think that luxury saved Martinez more than a few trips to the disabled list during his 18-year career, you're nuts. Just ask Paul Molitor, the first true designated hitter to make the Hall of Fame. Before 1991, his first full season as a DH, Molitor played more than 150 games in only 4 of his 13 seasons. As a DH, he surpassed that total four times in eight years. Molitor was a designated hitter for 1,174 games over his career, and it could be successfully argued that without DH years in 1993 (.332, World Series MVP), 1994 (.341), and 1996 (.341), Molitor had as much of a chance at the Hall of Fame as Dale Sveum did.

The DH saved Molitor's career. It gave Harold Baines a "position" from which he hit the majority of his 384 career home runs. It enabled several veteran stars to reach milestones that they might not have otherwise achieved had they continued to play the field—like Dave Winfield's 3,000 hits and Eddie Murray's 500th home run. In other words, it's a shortcut. It's a cheat. And while I'll respect the American League's continued support of the designated hitter, it doesn't mean that I have to like it or refrain from snickering every time I think about how that great five-tool ballplayer Dave Kingman hit 100 home runs as a DH in his last three major league seasons with Oakland . . . between the ages of 35 and 37.

Disco Demolition Night

"When you lose control and you got no soul / It's tragedy."

DO NOT misinterpret this entry as a slap in the face of Chicago DJ Steve Dahl and Chicago White Sox director of promotions Mike Veeck. When your aim is limited to attracting an immense crowd of drug-addled rock fans with a vow to explode a crate full of Donna Summer, ABBA, and Bee Gees records between games of a baseball doubleheader, eventually making a list of the worst ideas in sports history shouldn't be a concern—it should be a certainty.

I'm actually still in awe that they pulled it off and had the *cojones* to do so. Consider that 15,520 fans showed up at the last pre-Demolition home game at White Sox Park, while an estimated 90,000 filled the stadium, the concourse, and the parking lot chanting *Disco sucks!* the following evening. Consider that the Pied Piper who led these militant anti-disco hooligans—the Section Eight of Studio 54, apparently—was Dahl, a 24-year-old disc jockey who had transformed Chicago radio in less than two years with his unscripted banter and pro-"anything but disco" battle cry. Consider that the point of this thing was to blow up a crapload of vinyl in the middle of centerfield!

Fans storm the field at Chicago's White Sox Park on Disco Demolition Night, held on Thursday, July 12, 1979. (AP Photo/Fred Jewell)

On July 12, 1979, the White Sox had a doubleheader against the Detroit Tigers. Tapping into Dahl's counterculture movement—which was spreading during the same summer that the Pittsburgh Pirates were using a Sister Sledge song as their anthem—Veeck, 28 at the time, pitched the DJ with the Demolition Night idea after hearing the buzz that Dahl created by threatening to blow up a collection of dance discs at a local mall. Dahl agreed, although he predicted that the stunt would be executed in front of a nearly empty stadium.

No such luck. Dahl's acolytes flooded the box office, bringing in disco albums in exchange for a 98-cent ticket to the game. (Dahl worked for WLUP-FM 98.) Late-arriving fans were allowed into the stadium with their records because enough had been collected. None of the fans had been frisked, so records and other, more "medicinal" contraband were allowed in.

Let's clear up something: this notion of "fans." By all accounts, the crowd that filled the stadium on Demolition Night was there to get high, get rowdy, and get some visceral satisfaction out of watching a bunch of KC and the Sunshine Band records become hotter than the surface of the sun. They were not there to watch Detroit win the first game of the doubleheader, 4–1.

The game was littered with bouts of hooliganism. Records, golf balls, and beer were thrown on the field. A giant banner with a pot leaf on it was unfurled in the outfield, and observers alleged that a cloud of smoke accompanied it during the game. "I knew it wasn't going to be my finest moment when I saw that first guy slide down the foul pole," Veeck would tell ESPN.com some years later.

Between games, Dahl—wearing a military-style helmet—and his posse came onto the field in a jeep. A crate and a large Dumpster were in centerfield, filled with disco records. The crate was exploded first and then the dumpster—only the second blast used too much dynamite, sending mounds of debris into the air as the crowd roared.

As the pitchers for the next game began warming up, fans started spilling onto the field. Two slid into second base behind White Sox pitcher Ken Kravec, who had moved to the pitcher's mound after fireworks near the bullpen spooked him. Soon, thousands of fans began pouring out onto the field, and a full-on riot started. Home plate was stolen, as was the pitcher's mound. Outfield fires raged out of control. Police invaded the field en masse about a half hour into the pandemonium, and soon order was restored.

But the damage was done: Sparky Anderson, the Tigers' manager, had successfully lobbied the American League to force the White Sox to forfeit the game. Six people were injured while 39 were arrested. Dahl listened to the riot play out on a radio at a local Holiday Inn, while Bill Veeck—Mike's father and the owner of the Sox—tried his best to restore order, even singing "Take Me Out to the Ball Game" at one point.

From the perspective that any publicity is good publicity, this was a huge success for Veeck and for Dahl, who continued his dominant Chicago radio career for the next three decades. "It gave me a bond with the city that so far has been unbreakable," he told the *St. Paul Pioneer Press* in 2004. Veeck resigned after Demolition Night and was forced to rebuild his career in the minor leagues through his trademark outlandish promotions. He eventually came back to work for the Florida Marlins, the Tampa Bay Devil Rays, and, ironically, the Detroit Tigers. He also became an owner of several minor league franchises.

So it seems that some good came out of Disco Demolition Night. Some have even identified the event as a cultural touchstone—either a representation of youthful angst toward a souring economy or a symbol of mass homophobia in regard to disco music.

But the reason that the promotion was a horrible idea was that it was built on the premise of rage. It was a hate rally, without a shred of irony. They may have as well billed it as Angry Mob Night because that was the only result that something this acrimonious would produce. John Waters, the film director who has redefined bad taste about a dozen times during his career, once indirectly explained the difference between Disco Demolition Night and what the promotion could have been, in a lecture at the European Graduate School: "Nothing's funny if you make comedy about something you hate. It can be funny for about 10 minutes, but it doesn't really work unless you love what you're making fun of. I look up to bad taste because it's a freedom I don't have—I do care what people think. I don't sit on my front steps in my underpants and give people the finger when they go by."

Artificial Turf

The Grass Is Always Greener
When It's Fake

I REMEMBER sitting in the field boxes at Veterans Stadium in Philadelphia back in the early 1990s for a Phillies/Expos game. I remember this day for three reasons.

1. It was the day that the Phillie Phanatic, that miscreant mascot, swiped a 1969 New York Mets replica hat off of my noggin, tossed it on the ground, stomped on it with his stupid foam-filled feet, and placed it back on my head. The Philly fans roared with approval, but somewhere in that great dugout in the sky, Gil Hodges looked down and shed a solitary tear.

2. It was the day in which a portly young gentleman in the box next to us made lewd hand gestures and giggled uncontrollably whenever Phillies infielder Dickie Thon was announced at the plate.

3. It also marked the first time I had ever held a piece of artificial turf, which I leaned over the infield railing and scooped up off foul territory.

My first thought was "Who the hell would play on this crap?" It was slightly softer than a billiards table, with the same sort of fallacious green tint that suggests lush vegetation but merely masks its absence. It was sort of spongy, which I thought perfectly explained why routine infield grounders sometimes looked like an experiment in Flubber. It was the sort of unnatural surface that you might have expected to find at the Disneyland version of a baseball game: Mr. Toad's Wild Pitch, anyone?

I hate artificial turf. I hate the fact that grass has to be forever named "natural grass," as if God's great greenery could be anything but natural. I hate the fact that decades' worth of statistics can be called into question because players had a tactical advantage over their peers by playing on a rapid, impeccable track. I hate that there's actually something called "turf toe" in my life.

Turf toe, for the uninitiated, is a foot injury that occurs when an athlete pushes off repeatedly on a hard, unyielding surface—like artificial turf. If only turf's pernicious sins stopped at the feet; more than a few athletes have suffered significant injuries that would not have occurred on grass. In 1993, Wendell Davis of the Chicago Bears suffered ripped patella tendons in both knees on the infamous turf in the Vet against the Eagles when his feet got snagged on the carpet during a pass route. As Philadelphia quarterback Donovan McNabb told the Associated Press: "There's two things you can get hit by—our defenders or our stadium. They're both hard hits."

Football teams with artificial homefields began constructing their teams with that in mind (like the St. Louis Rams and the Indianapolis Colts, to name two). Average players in baseball became above average on turf. Hall of Fame second baseman Joe Morgan told *Sports Illustrated* that "on grass, you have to learn how to play the ball. On turf, all you have to do is get your glove down. I think it's made a lot of mediocre infielders look better than they are."

Artificial turf didn't exactly prove beneficial to the stadiums that housed it. The turf was called Chemgrass when it was invented in the 1960s; it was renamed AstroTurf after it replaced the botched grass experiment in the Astrodome for opening day, 1966. Turf suited the temperature-controlled dome well; not so in the cookie-cutter ballparks of the 1970s in Cincinnati (Riverfront Stadium), Pittsburgh (Three Rivers Stadium), and Philadelphia (the Vet). Without a dome shielding the sun, the fields' turf would heat up to 140 degrees on a sweltering summer day. The unsightly, uninspired architecture of these stadiums has also been blamed on the turf craze.

A backlash against artificial turf finally happened in the 1990s. Stadiums—such as Giants Stadium in New Jersey—switched to natural grass. In a 1998 survey, the NFL Players Association overwhelmingly voted (94.2 percent) that playing on turf increased their risk of injury. Stylish retro stadiums opened with more high-quality grass than what you'd find at the after-party of a Snoop Dogg concert. And for those stadiums that still yearned to go artificial, a new innovation was revealed: FieldTurf, which eschews some of the more injurious and perverting aspects of AstroTurf while maintaining its durability.

So, seeing as how things seem to be working out for the better, was AstroTurf a necessary evil we all had to endure? Nah . . . it sucked. And as former Phillies star Richie Allen once said, "If a horse won't eat it, I don't want to play on it."

The Glow Puck
FOX's Unfair Change Leaves Fans Unbalanced

AFTER SECURING broadcast rights to the National Hockey League for $155 million in 1994, the FOX network came to a startling conclusion: it had just paid out the ass for a regionally popular sport that didn't appeal to casual fans in non-hockey towns, especially on television. To quote one of the network's most beloved animated programs: *Aye carumba!*

Some observers thought that FOX was looking at its biggest financial disaster since Liz Taylor's *Cleopatra* if the NHL didn't attract viewers beyond the diehards. So, in an effort to entice more casual fans, the network that gave us *Married . . . with Children* and *Who Wants to Marry a Millionaire?* did the only thing that it really knew how to do well: it dumbed hockey down (OK, a little further down than Tie Domi already had).

The problem, in the eyes of FOX Sports executives, wasn't that most Americans didn't play hockey growing up or that, at the time, cities in the southern United States didn't have established franchises or didn't have hockey at all—not to mention the fact that most of the league's top players were named Sergei, Teemu, or Pavel. None of that mattered. They thought the problem was that viewers at home couldn't follow what was happening on their television screens . . . because they couldn't keep their eyes on that little black puck in the same way that they could a football or a basketball.

The World Hockey Association thought the same thing back in the 1970s and had some failed experiments with red- and blue-colored discs. FOX, however, was ready for Puck 2.0—not only would the biscuits be digitally colorized, but they would also *glow*, thanks to computer wizardry.

The glow puck was invented through the miracle of FoxTrax, which sounds like a bad *Charlie's Angels* rip-off ("Three foxes . . . hot on your tracks!") but was actually a state-of-the-art computer system in which a practically weightless, quarter-sized circuit board was implanted inside a regulation NHL puck. Twelve sensors around the outside of the puck emitted an infrared signal. Sensors on top of the glass tracked the puck around the rink, and a special "puck truck" outside the arena added computer-generated graphics.

The maiden voyage of the FOX glow puck was at the NHL All-Star Game on January 20, 1996, from Boston's Fleet Center. Hockey fans watched as the tiny black circle they were accustomed to following on television was consumed by an eerie blue fog, resembling either an old poker chip or the dot used to obscure the naughty bits on reality dating shows.

The cool part was that fans could follow the puck when it disappeared into the corners. The lame part was that the blue circle could never actually keep up with the puck. It was like being at a Rolling Stones concert where the spotlight never found Mick on stage. But FOX wasn't simply content with a somewhat distracting yet potentially helpful technology. No, sir—every time a player shot the puck over 70 miles per hour, a large red digital comet tail trailed behind it on the screen. A digital comet tail? This was not a hockey game; this was a video game! Why not just have an Italian plumber run out, eat a mushroom, and stomp some turtles between periods?

Had ice hockey, with over 100 years of tradition, finally sold its soul to American television? Football, baseball, and basketball certainly didn't need any graphical enhancement. Had the sport of Bobby Hull, Gordie Howe, and Jean Beliveau finally reached the point where it needed a puck that looked like it was just flown in from Chernobyl to attract viewers?

Reviews for the glow puck were mixed. Longtime fans were repulsed. Network executives ignored them, pointing to a jump in younger viewers and some favorable reviews from television critics. Despite the objections, FOX said that the glow would not go—but neither would the backlash. In 1998, after years of ridicule, the network finally dropped the blue dot, although it kept short blue and red streaks behind the puck whenever it was shot at a high velocity.

Due to a number of factors, ratings for the sport declined, and FOX was ready to hand hockey to ABC/ESPN for the league's next television deal. In a lame-duck 1999 season, FOX finally killed the glow puck during a massive budget slashing in its hockey coverage that also claimed the studio pregame show and three regional games.

The NHL moved to ABC/ESPN without glow pucks or comet tails, but fans still found a myriad of reasons to bitch about how the sport was being televised. FOX continued to add CGI bells and whistles to its sports coverage, including a successful application of FoxTrax to its NASCAR coverage. Viewers could follow their favorite drivers through digitally placed icons pointing to their respective cars, even in a tightly packed field.

But while the technology was eventually redeemed, the glow puck will forever be remembered as one of the most despised digital blunders of the 1990s. Well, at least until that remake of *Godzilla* came along . . .

The Bronze Medal
From Ancient Greece to Nagano, a Symbol of Futility

WHAT DOES the bronze medal mean to you? Top three? Runner-up to the runner-up? Close but no cigar?

How about . . . *loser*? Not only a loser but a bigger loser than the loser whom the winner defeated to become the winner.

The bronze medal is a trinket whose only purpose is to remind athletes that they're closer to fourth place than they are to first place. It wasn't always like this. In the first modern-era Olympic Games, held in Athens in 1896, only the first two finishers received awards. There wasn't a gold medal yet. First place received a silver medal and a crown of olive branches (a step down from ancient Greece, which used to exempt champions from paying taxes for an Olympiad). Second-place athletes were given a crown made of laurel and a medal made of bronze. That all changed at the 1904 Olympics, in which the gold medal was introduced as the ultimate prize for event champions. The silver was bumped down to second place. So the organizers now had all of these suddenly worthless bronzies on their hands, and third place began receiving some hardware as well.

Where did this historic change in Olympic policy take place, you ask? Where else? The United States—St. Louis, to be exact—the land where everyone's a winner. Who else votes on an all-American second team? What other nation hands out gold stars to every student in class, lest a single child begin questioning his or her own aptitude? Who else in the world could invent something as contemptuous as the "homecoming court"? (C'mon people—it's king and queen; everyone else is a nerd.)

Is the bronze medal really consistent with the bedrock virtues of athletic competition? Do athletes battle for the right to raise three fingers in the air?

Quick—when Affirmed beat Alydar in the Belmont Stakes in 1978 to win the Triple Crown, what horse completed the trifecta? When Magic Johnson's Michigan State team defeated Larry Bird and Indiana State for the 1979 NCAA national basketball championship, who won the tournament consolation game?

Without the bronze medal, no athlete would ever settle for anything less than best or second best on the world's greatest stage. The podium would be less crowded. Countries such as Mozambique, Belarus, and Sri Lanka would simply show up every four years for two ceremonies and the chance to be on TV.

Sure, the bronze medal has become an Olympic tradition, like the torch, the rings, and track-and-field athletes on horse tranquilizers. But back in 720 BC, so was competing in the nude.

Can you imagine how awkward fencing would be if *that* tradition was allowed to continue?

Selling Your Legend
Paying the Price for Greed

MONEY. SAMUEL Butler claimed the want of it was the "root of all evil." Ralph Waldo Emerson said that it "often costs too much." I prefer Honoré de Balzac's take: "Behind every great fortune, there is a crime."

When professional sports owners lust for great fortune, crimes are committed. Against the players. Against the franchise. Against the fans. And, most of all, against common sense and better judgment. Selling off Babe Ruth, Julius Erving, and Wayne Gretzky? Talk about your *Human Comedy* . . .

Theatrical producer Harry Frazee purchased the Boston Red Sox in 1916. At that point, George Herman Ruth was a star left-handed pitcher; he didn't see significant time as a position player until 1918. The following season, Babe Ruth was figuratively born, as the slugger knocked 29 home runs—at the time, a single-season record. Ruth had helped the Red Sox to four World Series titles in eight years. He was baseball's biggest—and largest—star. But in December 1919, Frazee sold Ruth to the New York Yankees; it was a move that prompted manager Ed Barrow to tell Frazee, "You ought to know that you're making a mistake." For 86 years, Red Sox fans heavyheartedly agreed.

Why did Frazee sell the Babe? Urban legend claims that it was to raise funds for his ultimately successful Broadway show *No, No Nanette*, which critics called "the happiest show in town" when it debuted in 1925. That story, however, isn't the whole story. Historians pinpoint several factors that influenced Frazee's decision to sell the Bambino. Money was one of them—World War I had taken its toll on both baseball and theater box offices, and the Yankees' deal of $125,000 in cash and a $300,000 loan was a boon for Frazee. Ruth's off-field behavior—boozy and boorish—was affecting the team. He was also a malcontent in the locker room.

Sure, it's a little Monday-morning quarterbacking to criticize this deal. Who knew selling the biggest superstar to hit the sport since Ty Cobb would result in a supernatural hex on an entire franchise—one that's probably funded the Bostonian psychiatric community for half a century? Who knew peddling Babe to the Bronx would be the reason for Bucky Dent and Bill Buckner's legs? But here's another question: *Who %$#& sells Babe Ruth to the Yankees?!*

When you sell out your fans by selling your legendary player, the stories behind the deals are never straight. Just as the Ruth deal was blamed on everything from *No, No Nanette* to the Babe's punching an umpire, the sale of Wayne Gretzky to the Los Angeles Kings offered conflicting tales from the Great One and Edmonton Oilers owner Peter Pocklington.

Pocklington was the man who transitioned the World Hockey Association's Oilers to the NHL in 1979—the same year that he inked an 18-year-old Gretzky to a contract. By 1988, the Oilers had compiled a streak of four Stanley Cups in five seasons. But that success hadn't sufficiently lined the pockets of Pocklington, so he began to seek out options to trade the most popular athlete in hockey history in exchange for players and cash. After flirtations with the Winnipeg Jets and Vancouver Canucks, Pocklington struck a deal with Los Angeles Kings owner Bruce McNall to send Gretzky to the

Golden State with Marty McSorley and Mike Krushelnyski in exchange for center Jimmy Carson, rookie Martin Gelinas, three first-round draft picks, and US$15 million, which at the time was close to $1 billion Canadian. (My math on the exchange rate might be a little off.)

Critics claimed that the deal was what Gretzky wanted, as his new bride—actress Janet Jones—desired to be closer to Hollywood. (Some newspapers and fans referred to her as the Yoko Ono of hockey.) Curmudgeonly hockey commentator Don Cherry slammed Gretzky for wanting to play in California, saying, "Not many people know L.A.'s even in the league." Plus, the Oilers could have lost Gretzky to free agency in three years.

The fans didn't buy it, accusing Pocklington of a money grab at the expense of the greatest player of all time. And Jones-Gretzky made it clear that her husband's anger with Pocklington was a major factor behind his agreement to the deal. "The key to everything that happened was an event five days after our wedding. Pocklington gave Los Angeles Kings owner Bruce McNall permission to take Wayne if he could do it," she told the *Edmonton Sun*. "The story of the trade as presented by Peter Pocklington is false. Pocklington is the reason Wayne's gone." Class act that he was, Pocklington claimed that Gretzky's tears at his final press conference were phony.

Edmonton won another cup in 1990 with remnants of Gretzky's teams. The Kings went to the Stanley Cup Finals in 1993 for the first time thanks to Gretzky, losing to the Montreal Canadiens in five games. The Great One ended his career as the leading goal, assist, and point scorer in the regular and postseasons. Edmonton, on the other hand, was in the red for most of its post-Gretzky years, and Pocklington sold the team in 1998. The Oilers barely avoided relocation to an American city . . . perhaps one in a balmy climate that Gretzky's time in Los Angeles helped lay the ground for, like Phoenix

(formerly Winnipeg and a team Gretzky became a managing partner for after his retirement.)

As dominating as Gretzky was during his tenure with the Oilers, Julius Erving was as equally dominating in his three seasons with the New York Nets. He won three consecutive MVP awards and led the team to a pair of American Basketball Association championships. This was in stark contrast with the previous years in the franchise's history, in which they basically found new and exciting ways to suck in the majority of their games. In 1976, the Nets entered the NBA along with Denver, San Antonio, and Indiana for a fee of $3.2 million apiece. The Nets had to pay an extra $4.8 million to the Knicks in order to "share" a territory and could not receive any television revenue for three seasons. Plus, Erving wanted a raise. Owner Roy Boe decided that the only course of action was to sell the biggest star in the team's history to the Philadelphia 76ers for $3 million. Erving went on to lead the Sixers to four NBA Finals and one NBA title, in 1983. The Nets went from ABA champions to a 22–60 cellar dweller in their first NBA season without Dr. J.

A group of season ticket holders successfully sued the team for a refund after Erving was traded. The following season, the Nets relocated to New Jersey.

The Coin Toss

There's a 50-50 Chance
I'm Right on This

THANKSGIVING DAY, 1998. The Pittsburgh Steelers and the Detroit Lions are tied 16–16 at the end of regulation and head into overtime. Referee Phil Luckett meets at midfield with representatives from each team to decide who receives the all-important first possession of the extra session. This decision will be made through the antithesis of the masochistic bodily sacrifice that the teams suffered through in the previous four quarters. It will be settled by the soft flip of a metallic coin.

Luckett asks Steelers running back Jerome Bettis to call it in the air. What happens next would go down in history as the most cringe-inducing controversy since Ralphie's mother "accidentally" broke his father's "major award" while dusting that fragile sexy leg lamp in *A Christmas Story*. Bettis claimed that he called tails. Luckett swore that he heard Bettis say "heads tails" and went with the first answer, giving the Lions the first offensive drive in overtime—one that ended the game on a field goal by Detroit's Jason Hanson. Bettis was adamant that he called tails. "I did not say 'heads tails,'" he demanded after the game. "That is a lie. That's a bald-faced lie."

Is this what football is about? Turning grown men into a bunch of toddlers arguing over a parlor game? Sports are about two things: athleticism and competition. Unless you consider thumbing through this book a physically arduous task, there's nothing athletic about flipping a coin. The coin toss also defies the competitive nature of sports; one team can never gain the advantage over the other to determine the outcome of a flip. It's all about chance, blind luck, a 50-50 prospect. You know that you're dealing with an inadequate decision-making mechanism when rock-paper-scissors provides a more thrilling match of wits.

The XFL didn't get much right, but it sure as hell knew what a joke it was to use a coin flip to determine offensive possession. Two players ran 20 yards to midfield and battled each other for the ball. Sure, all it needed was a banjo to completely make it look like a deleted scene from *Deliverance*. And yeah, Orlando Rage wide receiver Hassan Shamsid-Deen happened to separate his shoulder in the opening scrum of his team's inaugural game. But at least no one on the field thought he called "heads tails."

How ridiculous is the coin toss? Riddle me this: If the NFL determined the first possession of a Super Bowl overtime with two players spinning the giant wheel from *The Price Is Right*, would you be outraged? Or what if they had to pick a number between 1 and 100?

Could you imagine the uncontrollable rioting in western New York State if the Bills lost a fifth Super Bowl because their starting quarterback rolled craps?

Instant-Replay Abuse
After Further Review . . .

WHY DO people loathe instant replay? Perhaps it's because of the blown calls, game after game, by the invisible men in the booth. Or the fact that we can't see exactly what referees in the NFL are looking at under that television monitor blanket. (I always envisioned a video of the commissioner, swinging an antique watch side to side, slowly intoning, "You will award possession to the Cowboys . . . you will award possession to the Cowboys . . .") In any sport that uses it, the flow of the game is broken beyond repair by replay delays. Instant replay does what coaches get fined thousands of dollars for doing: it undermines the authority of the on-field officials.

But is it really all *that* bad? Isn't getting the correct call, especially in a "bang-bang" play that catches an official off guard, more important than having to wait an extra four minutes for a ruling? Instant replay does have its tangible benefits. It can correctly tell if a wide receiver had two feet inbounds while catching a ball (possession can be a little more dicey). You can use it to determine whether a puck crossed the goal line or, in rarer cases, whether the puck actually entered the net and bounced out. In those cases, instant replay is a valuable safeguard against human error in deciding the victor of a game.

But there's just too damn much of it. That's the problem. Consider the following as instances in which instant replay needs to instantly disappear:

- *Marking yardage in football:* Here are good intentions gone horribly wrong. While the use of video replay to see where a player's knee hit the ground or where he stretched the ball might seem like an admirable notion, there's one significant drawback: not one camera views the play from straight ahead or from ground level. Every replay is filmed with a camera on an angle, making a half-yard determination of where the ball should be spotted absolutely impossible. Besides, shouldn't a legion of on-field officials be in a better position to make such a call? Or is the league telling us that sometimes these calls are intentionally botched? Hmmmm . . .
- *Determining when time expires in the NBA:* Instituted in 2002 after several blown calls by referees at the end of important games, replay allows NBA officials to review last-second shots at the end of every quarter. Are two points scored at the end of the game more important than two points scored at 5 minutes, 33 seconds of the first quarter? Of course not—it's all the same value no matter when they're scored. So why not apply instant replay to the 24-second shot clock? Even though it would ruin the flow of the game, it would be more effective in determining the "real" winner. Or perhaps instant replay just has no place in professional basketball. Yeah, that's the ticket . . .
- *Crease violations in the NHL:* See an earlier chapter in this very book.
- *Whether the puck was kicked into the net:* This example is one of my favorites, because you're dealing with the "intent" of the player, in other words, whether a forward—in full stride to the crease—had the mind-set and reflexes to purposefully knock the puck in with his skate. Let me lay this example on you: if I were to kick you in the groin, one could safely assume that I was intending to do so. But what if I were merely kicking for kicking's sake and your groin just happened to be in the way? It doesn't change the fact that I kicked you in the groin, but it does call into question

301

whether I intended to do so. (Why does this suddenly sound like a speech from *The Matrix*?) Unless the NHL has Siggy Freud and a gypsy fortune-teller upstairs in the booth, intent is in the eye of the reviewer.

Furthermore, instant replay isn't used in situations in which it could—and should—be used. For example, what is the most replayed infraction during a football game on television? If you said pass interference, give yourself a gold star, buckaroo. The reason that it's shown so often is that the line between a penalty and an innocent play is so inconspicuous. Did the defender hit the receiver before the ball was there? Did the receiver push off the defender to catch the ball? Did either of them even make an attempt at the ball? These things are crystal clear on virtually any play with potential pass interference.

So why isn't it reviewable? One could argue that pass interference is the most game-altering call that a referee can make—a single call could take a team out of its own half of the field and into the other team's red zone. Other judgment calls—like the lamentable "bobbling the football" on catches—are handled through replay; the fact that interference isn't indicates that, yet again, referees simply want to maintain the luxury of subjectivity when the game is on the line; that is, they want to be guided by their own personal "script" for how the game should play out.

So in the end, instant replay itself is not one of the worst ideas in sports history. Its application, or lack thereof, is a different matter.

The Overtime Shootout

Undermines Every Facet of the Game in an Exciting Way

DECEMBER 28, 1958. Yankee Stadium. Johnny Unitas miraculously leads the Baltimore Colts downfield. With seven seconds left in the game, Steve Myrah's 13-yard field goal ties the NFL championship game with the New York Giants, 17–17, sending the crowd of 64,185 into a frenzy. Regulation time ends, and the most-watched televised title game at that point in history goes into sudden-death overtime. And we all remember what that meant, right?

Water-balloon fight!

The Colts' Raymond Berry splats one on Pat Summerall's back. The Giants' running back Frank Gifford hurls a gelatinous rubber orb at Unitas, but it splashes Charley Conerly, his own quarterback, when Johnny U. spins away. Who can forget that one-yard toss from Baltimore's Alan Ameche that saturates most of the Giants' defense to end the game? Final score: 24–17, Colts win!

Sure, it negated four quarters of thrilling action. And, OK, there really wasn't anything that resembled the strategy, defense, or team play that separates a sport like football from something like lawn darts. But water-balloon fights are *f-u-n* fun! And that's what matters most, right? *Fun?*

Washington Capitals forward Alex Ovechkin skates in against Tampa Bay's Sean Burke in an October 2005 shootout. (Greg Wyshynski)

No, of course not. Fun is dumb. Winning is not. Winning is everything. Winning is determining the correct victor in a fair and sensible manner. *That* is not dumb.

In reality, the Colts won that classic game in sudden-death overtime on an Ameche one-yard touchdown run—not in a water-balloon fight or a field-goal-kicking contest or a duel between Unitas and Conerly to see who could throw the most balls through a hanging rubber tire in 60 seconds. All of those scenarios might have provided more entertainment value than another quarter of football. One tiny little problem: *They aren't football!*

Why don't extra-inning games end with home run derbies? Because they're fun, but they're not baseball. Why don't overtime games in the NBA end with three-point shooting competitions? Because they're fun, but they're not basketball.

But soccer, ice hockey, and field hockey—to name just a few offenders—decide a winner in their respective sports with a methodology alien to the previous halves or periods that the teams just completed. In hockey and soccer, the game is reduced to one offensive player versus a goaltender. In hockey, that means disregarding 10 other hockey players that had factored into every play; in soccer, it's ignoring 20 other players who were on the field during the rest of the game. Overtime shootouts have such an infinitesimal relevance to the games they finish that the question becomes, why not just have a water-balloon fight instead?

Strategy is replaced with reflexes and blind luck. An entire game's worth of actions, reactions, and adjustments is filtered down into whether someone's going to guess left or right. It's a joke to think that 120 minutes of intense World Cup soccer can be reduced to a series of unguarded kicks on the goalkeeper that don't involve a single completed pass. Offense and defense decide champions; not glorified skills competitions. Shootouts are an insult to team sports.

In a way, though, shootouts are sort of a backhanded compliment to soccer and hockey. Both sports are such wars of attrition that they don't fit into the cookie-cutter, made-for-TV world of modern-day sports such as basketball or football; hence, something had to be invented to end the games prematurely. (Baseball games, of course, are the exception. We fully understand that like seasons of *The Sopranos* and orgasms, the good ones are just going to take a little longer to finish.)

But what makes soccer and hockey remarkable—their grueling physical nature—is not found within the shootout. Take the 1987 Patrick Division semifinal classic between the New York Islanders and the Washington Capitals. Fans from both teams still talk about that four-overtime Game 7 because, in the end, the players left every ounce of their strength and stamina on the ice. After the game, Kelly Hrudey, the Islanders' goalie, was quoted as saying, "I was too tired to have any emotion. It gets to the point where your body doesn't feel anything and your mind plays the game. It was a once-in-a-lifetime thing." And to think, Hrudey could have simply faced three shooters, four overtimes earlier, and called it a night.

So why is the overtime shootout the worst idea in sports history? It's so damn sexy, that's why. It's a temptress; the blast of an air horn following a goal its siren song. The shootout is an admirable concept, from an entertainment standpoint. You showcase your stars, decide a winner, and everyone goes home satisfied.

Some of the most memorable games in sports history were decided on penalty kicks or shootouts. The U.S. National Women's Soccer team won the 1999 World Cup on its own soil with Brandi Chastain's penalty kick turned striptease against China. Argentina ousted England with penalty kicks in a 1998 World Cup round of 16 game in France. Peter Forsberg's shootout goal gave Sweden the gold medal for men's ice hockey in a 1994 Winter Olympic final and landed him on a postage stamp. Yet in all three cases, drama was manufactured through an artificial mechanism for determining a winner. Think of those overtime classics that didn't need gimmickry to burn their images into our mind's eye. Christian Laettner, 1992 East Regional final, catching a court-long inbounds pass and hitting that turnaround shot from the top of the key to eliminate Kentucky. The Boston Celtics, 1976 NBA

Finals, fighting off the assiduous Phoenix Suns, who forced triple overtime on an 18-foot jumper by Gar Heard with one tick left in the second extra session. Carlton Fisk, 1975, willing his 12th-inning home run ball fair as he galloped to first base in Game 6 of the Red Sox's World Series against Cincinnati. Those games and countless others offered something that a shootout never could or never will: spontaneity. As soon as a soccer or hockey game reaches penalty kicks or shots, fans know the end is near—whether it's six skaters or six kickers, it's just a matter of time. In any other overtime format, we do not know when the end will arrive, nor do we know how or why.

Yet there's no question that a sport like soccer might need artificial means to end a stalemate. By a sixth overtime, players would be so fatigued that they'd look like two teams' worth of George Romero zombies (*Game of the Dead*?). So if a shootout isn't the answer, what is? Thinking specifically about the World Cup—where shootouts really tarnish a champion—I offer two alternatives. What about giving teams five corner kicks apiece? At least then you'd add in elements of strategy and, more important, defensive players. Or simply go back to the way things were when the cup tournament was much smaller: replay the championship game a week later, should the title match reach a stalemate. Same teams, round two, winner take all? Television wouldn't love that?

In hockey, the best alternative to the shootout is to just play the game, television time constraints be damned. A four-on-four, 20-minute extra session will result in at least one goal being scored more often than not; it's just that the NHL hasn't ever tried that format—or even a three-on-three overtime format to see if either could successfully eliminate ties from the standings.

The fact that even the most fervent advocates of the regular-season shootout cringe at the idea of it being used in the postseason speaks volumes about its inadequacy. The longest NHL playoff game in history went six overtimes in 1936, the equivalent of nearly three complete games. In the modern NHL, the lengthiest playoff games run five overtimes at most. The spectacle of two completely drained teams battling deep into the early morning for their playoff lives is something that a shootout could never replicate.

Furthermore, the shootout rewards someone that the majority of fans loathe: the highest bidder. Shootouts indemnify teams with individual, and typically high-priced, talent rather than those that succeed with homogenous chemistry. You know who would love the shootout? George Steinbrenner. That should be all you need to hear.

In over a century's worth of bad ideas in sports, overtime shootouts—while tantalizing—are clearly the worst because they're an insult to the very games they end.

ABOUT THE AUTHOR

GREG WYSHYNSKI is an award-winning sportswriter and columnist who specializes in blending humor with insight in covering professional, collegiate, and amateur sports. Since 1999, he has served as the executive sports editor for The Connection Newspapers, a Northern Virginia newspaper chain. He has received thirty-eight Virginia Press Association awards, including four first-place citations for sports column writing. Wyshynski has also served as the senior editor for *SportsFan Magazine* and its website, sportsfanmagazine.com. Wyshynski currently resides in Ashburn, Virginia.